Maroon

Jackie Smith

How the devil are you?
Red, of course!

To
John
Blue Skies & miles of smiles
with love
from
Jackie Smith
D1113
WORLD CHAMPION
XX

British Library Cataloguing in Publication Data
A catalogue record for this book is available from the British Library.

ISBN 978-0-9957502-1-0

Printed by Salisbury Printing Company Limited, Salisbury
www.salisburyprinting.co.uk

Foreword by Edward Gardener

Colonel Ed Gardener

I met Jackie in the early 70s when she joined the Red Devils. In 1964 I had been lucky enough to raise and command the Parachute Regiment Freefall Team (later called the Red Devils) – it was just a case of being in the right place at the right time. Although I only held the appointment for one year, other military commitments and postings permitting I continued to 'guest jump' with the team for many years, did lots of displays with Jackie and we have remained friends ever since.

She started her parachuting career as an attractive and quite shy young WRAC soldier (she used to come and baby sit our children, I think partly to escape the rather austere surroundings and disapproving atmosphere in the WRAC barracks where she had to live). She quickly showed great ability, courage and determination, not only in making such rapid progress in a male dominated sport, but also in getting herself accepted as an equal by such a daunting team. Nothing was made easy for her – particularly by some of the conservative military hierarchy who seemed determined to put every obstacle in her way. But fortunately, with some assistance in the right places, she overcame all these hurdles and continued to become arguably one of the greatest sport parachutists in the world, male or female. As you will discover in the following pages, her achievements were legion and set a record of which anyone could be proud. Yet she has never lost her kindness, modesty and sense of humour.

I consider it a great honour to have been asked by Jackie to write these few words of introduction to her story. I would commend it to anyone whether or not they are parachutists. She hasn't pulled her punches and tells it – warts and all!

Edward Gardener
UK D113, US D1922.

Foreword by Doug Peacock

Jackie is, beyond doubt, the First Lady of British parachuting. She made her first jump on a basic course at Netheravon in March 1971, and thereafter events evolved rapidly as her obvious talent and dedication was quickly recognized. Three months and thirty-three descents later she made her first display jump with 9 Squadron Royal Engineers demonstration team and then went on to win the Novice Event at the Army Parachute Championships. Within a month she was training with the Parachute Regiment Display Team, the Red Devils and was seconded to DZ duties with them for the rest of the season. Early the next year, purely on merit she was taken on the strength of the team as a full member and was awarded the famed Regimental Red Beret a year later.

In 1974 she became British Ladies National Champion in the Style and Accuracy events and was selected for the British Team at the World Parachuting Championships at Szolnok in Hungary. At that time I was team coach and became immediately impressed by her ability and dedication. Two years later she retained her Style title at the Nationals and again competed in the WPC in Rome. In 1978 she was first placed lady overall at the British Nationals and was an automatic choice for the British Team at the 14th WPC in Zagreb. This was to become the zenith of her career as she became World Accuracy Champion, making history in the process by becoming the first competitor ever, male or female, to score ten consecutive dead centres in ten rounds at a World Championships. Further to emphasise her versatility, the following year she won a Silver medal at the World Formation Skydiving Championships as a member of the 4-way Symbiosis team.

Jackie has chronicled her parachuting career with candour and with humour; relating her time as the first female ever to become a member of any military parachute display team worldwide, and continuing with her subsequent concurrent and highly successful seasons in World competition and her life in the USA as a display jumper. This is the inside story of a professional parachutist which will strike an immediate chord with all jumpers and will provide the layman with a unique insight into a life defined by freefall jumping. Character, bravery and an all-pervading sense of humour shine throughout this narrative; a true reflection of the lady herself.

I consider it a pleasure and a privilege to have been known as her friend.

Doug Peacock AFM, RAF (Retd.)

Flying the Nest

They say that a journey of a thousand miles begins with the first step. My incredible journey began with a monumental step that took me into the Army Recruiting Office on Linthorpe Road, Middlesbrough way back in 1968 when I was fifteen years old. A naïve native of what was then the North Riding of Yorkshire, I dreamed of becoming a physical training instructor in the British Army and wherever the inspiration or courage came from to sign on the dotted line for Queen and country I have absolutely no idea.

I grew up on a council estate with two brothers and two sisters, was the fourth of five children to Mam and Dad, Ted and Mary. Childhood memories are of a freezing cold house, lino floors, a pantry colder than any fridge we never had, and Jack Frost's artwork on the inside of the windows every morning throughout winter. We never, ever, locked the doors, and visitors to the house were classed as family even if they weren't directly related. Everyone knew everyone and I even knew local dogs and cats' names. After school and weekends I played outside with the gang of boys who lived close by on Bevanlee Road and played funkies (dare) jumping the wide stretches of the Beck which ran along the back of my house. We built dens, played hide and seek, rolled marbles in the gutters, jumped off the three air-raid shelters by the boys' school, made rope swings around the lamp-posts, went apple raiding and rode the gypsy's horses bareback in the top fields. Bath night was once a week on a Sunday so for the rest of the week everyone I knew was dirty and grubby but we didn't care, we were having fun in the big wide world outside. On Mondays everyone at school was squeaky clean and shiny but as the week progressed we got dirty again and most probably smelled to high heaven before Sunday's bath day came around. The street lights were our curfew and if I got into trouble at school I didn't dare tell my parents otherwise I'd get a clip around the ear from Mam then a warning of "Woe betide when your Dad gets home!" We had nowt and expected nowt and looking back now I realise we had it all. During my senior school years, I excelled in sport being keen as mustard in competitive school and county swimming, badminton and rounders and also pursued the Duke of Edinburgh's Award at bronze, silver and gold level in Service (to the community), Skills (I chose Arts and Craft, Painting), Nature and the Environment, Physical Recreation… participating in ball sports, volleyball, netball, athletics; running, long jump, javelin, diving, swimming, trampolining and judo. I swam for my school at inter-school championships and was the only female to ever dive from the high diving board from the age of 12 onwards.

From inside the train carriage doorway I looked down at my Mam who was standing on the platform and she handed me a brown envelope containing the War Department's travel warrant, my one-way ticket to London and the connecting journey to Guildford in Surrey. With one last hug and kiss, she ran her fingers through my fringe, pinched my cheek and said, "You've got wanderlust in your veins, do more than just exist and enjoy the adventure!"

Mam had left home at the age of 14 to work as a chambermaid for the Wilberforce family, William Wilberforce being the leader of the movement to abolish the slave trade, and from her humble beginnings had experienced a downstairs working lifestyle for her upstairs employers. At the age of 15 her employer invited her into his light aircraft for her first and only flight and she sampled first-hand how the other half lived. Mam was well aware there was a better life out there for me than my home town of South Bank could offer. Little did any of us know that my lifestyle was to take on a different meaning of upstairs; a life between clouds and dreams where I've lived and worked punching holes with my parachute in the skies.

It was the first time I'd ever been away from home and, although nervous, was very excited to be joining the Women's Royal Army Corps to become a soldier. Leaving my safe harbour and ordinary life in a small northern town to venture off into uncertainty was the bravest thing I ever did and who'd have guessed at the fairy-tale adventure ahead of me. Unfortunately, Dad wasn't there to see me off but as the main breadwinner in the family he couldn't just take the day off work, it wasn't the done thing then. I think if he had been there to see me off I might not have caught the train as the previous evening I'd found him sitting on the stairs sobbing uncontrollably, the thought of his little girl flying the nest was too emotional an event in his life.

Perched on the edge of should I go or should I stay I took flight and have never looked back.

After a laboriously slow journey, the train came to a halt at London King's Cross station where its cargo of passengers spewed out onto the platform into a fast flowing river of people hurrying towards the exit. The ticket attendant checked my Army Travel Warrant and pointed to the London Underground advising I needed to travel to Waterloo main line station to catch a connecting train to Guildford. I was lost in a sea of people who all appeared to know where they were going, so like a sheep I went with the flow down the steps and into the network of underground tunnels.

On board the subterranean sardine can and wedged tightly between the other passengers I came face to face with the first soldier I'd ever seen in real life.

Noticing my brand new army suitcase, the soldier asked, "Where are you going?"

"Guildford", I said, "I'm joining the Army today and haven't a clue how to use the underground system to find my way to Waterloo".

"Where are you going?" I asked.

"White City" he said. "It's in the other direction to Waterloo but it's no problem, I'll take you there!"

The train sped through the dark tunnels rocking and wheezing, everyone huddled tightly and swaying awkwardly in unison until the brakes screeched to a halt. My soldier escort offered his hand to carry my heavy suitcase and in a tide of people we shuffled towards the exit moving slowly through the network of tunnels where I followed directly behind him, footstep for footstep, up the stairs and escalators. At eye level in front of me as we climbed the stairs was the pertest bum I'd ever seen, its firm, buff, round and chuchi shape was emphasised by a maroon belt around his trim waist.

On a scale of 1 to 10 I'd say his bum scored a Fwoar Factor 15. Other than his bum I really didn't notice too much more about him apart, that is, from his twinkling blue eyes, high cheek-bones, chiselled jawline, white glinting teeth, sun-kissed skin, broad athletic build and oh-so-firm bulging biceps which filled the sleeves of his camouflage jacket. At the top of his right sleeve, a winged badge was neatly sewn, below it a black square flash with an embroidered red X. He was a member of 10 Para (Volunteers) but I was unaware of that at the time, being ignorant of all things military.

Arriving at my departure platform we hurriedly exchanged scribbled addresses and said our goodbyes before I rushed off in the direction of my connecting train. As I boarded the train the piece of paper with his name and address fell between the carriage and the platform and not able to retrieve it never had the opportunity to write and thank the soldier. I was totally clueless as to his regiment or the association of his head-wear, cap-badge or uniform but on that day he really was my knight in shining armour, or should I say, Airborne Denison Smock.

You're in the Army Now

A stocky, uniformed female energetically stomped towards me, her shiny black steel-tipped flat and unattractive shoes click-clacked with authority on the concrete platform at Guildford train station. The friction of her inner thighs adorned with issue bullet-proof stockings rubbed together making a fizz, fizz, sound announcing her arrival in front of me. Standing squarely before me and practically nose to nose the female bellowed, "Name?" with such force my hair lifted from my forehead.

"Blimey!" I thought, "There's no need to shout! I'm not deaf", but not daring to challenge her abruptness answered naively, "Jacqueline Smith, but you can call me Smudge".

With thumb and finger on her chin she gave me a wry smile that only angry Corporals can then glanced down at her millboard and ran her finger up and down the lists until she found my name.

"From now on you will be known as Smith 161, not Jacqueline nor Smudge, and if I ask you a question you reply to me as Corporal. Understand?"

"Yes!" I said.

"Yes WHAT?" she barked.

"Yes Corporal!"

That was to be the first of many hairdryer treatments throughout my basic training.

With a sharp intake of air, I realised that moment was the start of my new life, the civilian I had previously been was no longer, I'd entered the reprogramming process and my identity was a military number.

The journey to the WRAC barracks at Queen Elizabeth Park, Guildford was exciting as we rocked and swayed inside a canvas-covered Army Bedford 4-Tonner that cold April evening. Arriving at the barracks we jumped from the vehicle's high tailgate assembling into groups with other new recruits who'd arrived earlier in the day and formed shambolic, disorganised three-line squad formations. We were a mixed bag of shapes and sizes, a myriad of personalities and accents from varying backgrounds and all wearing the 'groovy' trends of the day, shift dresses, mod miniskirts, go-go boots, high platform shoes, flared trousers and some daringly tight hot-pants.

Basic training was the biggest shock to my system where intense discipline, strict routines and lack of sleep became the norm. Us new recruits learned so many new personal skills and developed into stronger characters along the way to achieving our united goal of becoming soldiers. It certainly wasn't an easy ride being remodelled into someone new but at the end of basic training, those who made the grade became stronger and self-disciplined females, and not only were we all as smart as carrots but squeaky clean, hygienic and smelled fresher too.

The most mentally challenging and feared exercise in training was having to go into the Gas Chamber. Before entering we were shown how to fit the protective gas mask and then taken in large groups into the chamber which was dark and filled with white, foggy, CS gas. The sergeant in charge touched each person's shoulder in turn when we took in a deep breath, closed our eyes, lifted the mask from the face and recited regimental number, rank and name before filing out towards the exit. It was impossible not to breath in the CS gas which gave a sharp burning and stinging sensation to the lungs and obviously, we had to open our eyes to see where the door to exit was. Immediately, we started coughing, our eyes filled with water and it was very hard resisting rubbing them which was the worst thing to do. Outside, we sat or lay on the floor in coughing and choking heaps with streaming eyes and noses resisting the urge to rub our stinging eyes. It was most comforting to be told there was to be no group photograph taken afterwards as the entire squad looked like red-eyed zombies and representing the dead!

During basic training, some girls cried and crumbled, suffering traumatic homesickness, pining for creature comforts or a comforting hug from family, but everyone pulled together lifting those individuals who lost their motivation and were about to throw in the towel. We took on the daily challenges enthusiastically as a team, block cleaning, ironing, bed-making, marching, bulling our shoes, room inspections and PT. Some couldn't hack it and decided Army life wasn't for them but it never crossed my mind to give up and return home because I enjoyed the structure and discipline the new life gave me. I was going big; I wasn't going home! The Army introduced me to a totally different lifestyle from the one I'd left behind and I absolutely loved every minute of it, apart that is from cleaning the toilets and sinks with bleach and a toothbrush. The army taught me a new word in 'ablutions' and importantly, I learned a very important lesson, how to wipe my bum correctly. Who'd have guessed there was a right and wrong way of using 'Government Property' Izal toilet paper. Use the rough side and you wiped; use the shiny side and you ended up spreading it.

With the first four weeks of training under our belts, those who had achieved the grade and not back-squadded were allowed some freedom to venture out beyond the confines of the camp's fence. Before we were given that long-awaited freedom however, we were advised, or should I say 'cautioned' if we intended venturing to the nearby town of Aldershot.

"Why?" we asked in unison.

Because Aldershot was the home of the British Army's Parachute Regiment and Paras it seemed had somewhat of a reputation.

Did we heed the warnings? Certainly not! We'd been bottled up in a strict military regime for four weeks and in typical defiance tarted ourselves up to the nines with pan-cake slap, lashings of mascara, dressing for the first time in a month in our best civvies attire. In a heady cloud of Charlie and Tweed perfume, we headed off, Aldershot bound, to find out for ourselves what these Paras were all about.

"Aldershot, Aldershot! This is Aldershot!" came the announcement over the speaker as the train slowly approached the station. We'd arrived! The air filled with chatter and squeals of excitement as we made our way onto the platform to cross the bridge to the exit. Outside the station we noticed a café, the Top Hat Café, where we piled in, en masse, asking directions to where we might find some Paras. The bemused café owner smiled wryly and pointed towards Station Road.

"Go to the end of the road and you'll find the Naafi Roundabout Club directly in front of you and in there you'll find all the Paras you could ever dream about!" he said. As we left his cafe we heard him cackling in a deep throaty and dirty Sid James-type-of cackle – in our cloud of naivety we must have looked like lambs to the slaughter!

We arrived at the Roundabout Club, pushed open the heavy swing doors and made our entrance only to stop dead in our tracks at a scene of carnage. It was as if we'd stepped into the Rocky film set with punch-ups (milling) here, there and everywhere. Young Paras-in-the-making, were knocking fifty shades of brown stuff out of each other. Their comrades-in-arms gathered around each fight shouting encouragement, egging on the fighters, cheering loudly every time a punch planted an opponent. The floors were covered in blood, snot, vomit and beer, the air a pungent cocktail of testosterone, teen spirit and cigarette smoke. Bravely (or was it stupidity), we headed upstairs to the disco squeezing past a couple more fights, ducking and diving to avoid being laid out ourselves by stray swinging punches intended for their bloody-nosed targets. It was the same scene upstairs as it was downstairs, the only difference being the deafening music and flashing disco lights which added more drama and colourful visuals to those fighting on the dance floor.

The place was heaving and it was impossible to get to the bar. With nowhere to park our handbags to dance around we made a command decision to get the hell out of there as quickly as possible and head for another pub. As we made our way down the circular stairway the loud music petered into silence and two older and bigger Paras, both called Taff, were having a serious head-to-head with each other. The stockier of the two bellowed a long 'Aaarrrrrgh' then demonstrated an amazing feat of strength by picking up the jukebox before throwing it out the window. Everyone stood in silence until the jukebox smashed loudly on the ground outside when the fist-fest inside resumed so we scarpered out of there as fast as we possibly could.

Across the road and roundabout was a small, quiet-looking, pub so we headed inside expecting a more civilized atmosphere than the hellhole we'd just escaped from. Big mistake! As we entered we were hit by a pungent burning smell. We should have taken that smell as our cue to leave, but instead we pushed through the crowd towards the bar only to find a half-naked hairy-arsed paratrooper performing one of the Parachute Regiment's hallowed traditions, the 'Dance of the Flaming Arseholes' to encouraging cheers from the airborne fraternity and whoever else had dared to venture into the pub. The 'piss' artiste (he was very drunk) waddled between two arbitrary points while bent over with his pants around his ankles, a lighted, rolled-up piece of newspaper, held in place by a tightly clenched bum. He shuffled from the start line to the finish line without dropping the flaming 'torch' while his compatriots chanted the song "Haul 'em down you Zulu Warrior, Haul 'em down you Zulu Chief, Chief, Chief, Chief". The artiste obviously lost concentration and relaxed his clenched bum which lost its grip and the flaming newspaper dropped into his pants. Before the flames could do too much damage they were doused, reluctantly, in beer. His penalty for failing to complete the dance correctly was to perform the routine all over again when he proceeded to roll up a new piece of paper to again stick up his bum. It was a rite of passage within the Regiment where everyone participated to gain acceptance and strengthen the brotherhood ties by the age-old adage of shared absurdity. The pub reeked of singed bum fluff and I doubt for one minute that the 'artiste' that evening ever needed to invest in a sack, back or crack wax. The scene of burning bum to tribal chant was hilariously funny to witness and we laughed and laughed, but decided to leave the entertainment for fear the establishment might burn down.

Approaching the far end of Station Road, we encountered another group of Paras gathered around some more fighting, the air was filled again with encouraging cheers and swearing. With the railway station in sight we took off our shoes and ran like the wind escaping any unwanted attention, not that anyone noticed us anyway as they were far too occupied cheering on the fight. Not until the train pulled away from the platform and out of the station did we let out a sigh of relief, but then burst into uncontrollable laughter for the whole journey back to Guildford, not believing what we'd just witnessed in Aldershot. It was the most memorable night in my life!

With aspirations of becoming a Physical Training Instructor I and other prospective PTIs initially joined another regiment or corps for a year to gain military experience before attending the Army School of Physical Training (ASPT) located at Hamersley Barracks, Aldershot. I elected to join the Royal Signal Regiment and trained in military communications and procedures at Catterick, North Yorkshire.

At the end of Royal Signals training each recruit's 2-year posting was announced and names were called out alphabetically. I was way down the list at 'S' and had an agonising wait to find out where my posting would be. Others before me were given exciting sunshine postings to places such as Malaysia, Hong Kong, Germany and Cyprus and squeals of excited chatter filled the air after each announcement. I began to get sucked into the excitement, that is until eventually, my name was called.

"Smith, 161" shouted the Sergeant.

With bated breath, heart beating wildly, I was barely able to contain myself in anticipation. The Sergeant's mouth opened and to my horror the word "Aldershot" came out. Devastated, my heart gave a hard thud and for a few seconds stopped beating. A loud, collective groan of disapproval filled the room then everyone around commiserated, patted my back offering comfort saying, "Oh, too bad you're going to Aldershot, that really sucks!" I was the youngest in the troop and because I wasn't yet 17 and 10 months was too young to be given an overseas posting.

As a troop we marched towards the accommodation block, everyone else elated with high spirits; meanwhile I mooched along, just about in step, my arms going through the motions of swinging but lacking in vitality while reflecting on that oh-so-memorable night in Aldershot.

Aldershot, Aldershot, this is Aldershot

My first posting and place of employment, was with 3 Squadron, 10 Signal Regiment based in Headquarters South East District, Steele's Road, Aldershot, my accommodation just a short distance away in the newly built Duchess of Kent Barracks. The all-female accommodation had modern facilities which were in direct contrast to the accommodation at Catterick Camp where I shared basic facilities in a room with 15 others in a wooden Nissan hut. At the new 'digs' four girls shared a room, each having her own bed-space with 2'6" bed, wooden locker and chest of drawers. It was far less regimented and relaxed in the new working environment and we were even allowed to adorn our walls with a couple of photographs to give a homelier feel.

I loved my new army life and when I wasn't working, sleeping, or eating I was participating in sport, swimming in the military pool on Queens Avenue, working out in the gym or playing badminton and squash at Depot, The Parachute Regiment's Browning Barracks where the military blokes (I was the only female) offered to give me a good thrashing. I'm sure if I left the sexual innuendo door open ever so slightly they'd have come crashing through like a stampede of stallions. When it came to the badminton I certainly wasn't an easy push-over having played most of my badminton matches at league standard before joining the army and took great delight giving my opponents a run for their money making them run around the court like headless chickens and returned the banter with, "Come on then! Where's this thrashing you promised?" Within a couple of weeks, I made some wonderful friends at Depot Para and Major Geoffrey Norton, 2IC Depot the Parachute Regiment, asked if I'd partner him in a mixed doubles team to represent The Parachute Regiment in inter-unit matches and also at the Inter-Service Badminton Championships at Worthy Down. We established a good team rapport and later on in my skydiving career it was Major Norton along with the Regimental Colonel, Joe Starling, who became instrumental in my successful posting to the Red Devils Parachute Team.

At the far end of Queens Avenue, behind the Army School of Physical Training, I saw parachutes for the very first time. A large, silver, hydrogen-filled balloon with metal-framed cage suspended underneath, rose into the air to 800ft lifting four paratroopers and an RAF Parachute Jump Instructor. The balloon was tethered by a winch cable on a stationary, green Army Bedford vehicle, and what better place to lay down but directly underneath the balloon to watch the action going on overhead. One by one the paratroopers jumped in quick succession from the cage, feet first in a standing-up position. I watched with gob-smacking awe as each of them fell towards me, so close I could virtually see the depth of their DMS boots sole-tread. Drab olive-green round parachutes opened sharply then closed briefly, as if breathing, before totally inflating again and drifting to the ground. The paratroopers landed all around me, their feet hitting the ground with a 'whoomp' when they rolled over with their feet and knees firmly together in a parachute landing fall. It was amazing! Never in my life had I seen anything like it and just the experience of watching them made me buzz with excitement. In my wildest dreams I could only imagine what it might feel like to actually jump myself and heard myself saying out loud, "Wow oh wow! I've got to have some of that!"

Up 800ft, 4 men jumping

Pre Demo

First Jump

Early in March 1971 Part 1 orders were pinned to the notice board in my accommodation block and I and two other girls had been successful in securing a place on a basic parachute course. The other two females accompanying me were Private Tina Hayward (now Siddall) and LCpl Rowena Bazelle, and we were to join twenty other course students from the Junior Parachute Company scheduled for 28th March 1971 at the Joint Service Parachute Centre at Netheravon. It was the day before my 19th birthday and I couldn't think of a better present to look forward to opening, a parachute, above my head.

For the few weeks leading up to the 28th March, Staff Sergeant Instructor (SSI) Derek Thorne took us through parachute ground training in Browning Barracks' gymnasium where we packed and unpacked our parachutes (canopies) until the cows came home. The equipment was cumbersome, surplus US military B4 backpacks weighing in the region of 40lbs and the harness was bare webbing (no padding), covered in hardware, D-Rings, alligator clips and snap ejectors. We laid out the canopies, untangled lines, carried out line checks, flaked and neatly folded the nylon material, pulled the long cotton deployment sleeve over the immaculately folded canopy, neatly stowed the suspension lines using 'bungees' (elastic bands) and attached a long static-line to the top of the canopy. With so much bulk to squeeze into the parachute container we students found it nigh on impossible to flatten the two metal coiled-sprung pilot chutes, keep in place and close the container by inserting the four metal ripcord pins into the closure cones. When Derek demonstrated how to close the pack he made it look so easy but for the rest of us it wasn't quite that simple. We struggled to follow his example and slipped the full length (and back) of the highly polished gymnasium floor, grappling with the containers like Sumo wrestlers, to no avail. Those damned coiled spring pilot chutes escaped the backpack and sprung up like Jack-in-the-Box. Despondent, some lost their rag completely and brute force and ignorance set in, thumping and punching the rig, cursing, sweating buckets and most edging towards emotional breakdown. Every one of us failed miserably in our attempts and called Derek for help. He knelt down, took hold of a container, pinned it between his knees and closed it with minimal effort. In unison, everyone shook their heads in disbelief. Smirking like a Cheshire cat Derek said, "There! How easy was that? It's not about strength, it's all about technique!"

Determined to close my rig without asking for help I packed parachutes at every opportunity, during my lunch break from work, every evening and all weekend packing sometimes up to ten static-line and freefall rigs a day leading up to the start of the parachute course. Derek was right, it was all about technique using not an ounce of brute force and ignorance and using his example I learned his method until I could pack my parachute blindfolded.

Packing a C9LL Canopy

JSPC Netheravon

At very early o'clock, our 4-tonne tarpaulin-covered Bedford arrived at Netheravon Camp on the edge of Salisbury Plain after a long, cold and breezy journey. We checked into the guardroom and the males on the course were directed to their accommodation blocks, old single-storey Nissan huts, located a short distance away. There was no accommodation for females on Netheravon camp and no camping allowed or bunkhouse facilities either so arrangements were made to transport the girls back and forth to the WRAC block located about five miles away at Larkhill Camp.

Derek called a briefing for everyone, jump students, parachute instructors and pilot, to be on the DZ, ready to go, at 04.45hrs the following morning. The weather forecast was favourable and a parachute programme was a positive 'goer'. With jump manifests in his hands listing names in jump order for the next day, Derek announced the first lift. No prizes for guessing who number one on lift number one was to be! Yours truly!

At the crack of Sparrow's fart the next morning, 27th March 1971, Derek shouted, "get your backsides into gear, kit up! Go! Go! Go!" It was a 'fetch-me-my-brown-trousers' moment and instantly, my bladder went into nervous 'pee-now-and-pee-often' mode. The ground training room fell quiet, the silence was deafening, and we anxiously put on our harnesses as we'd practised over and over again in training. The male species amongst us concentrated on gonad protection drills delving deep into their underpants to position their meat and veg well clear of the tight harness leg-straps, avoiding any possibility of nut crushage when the parachute opened.

The first three aircraft lifts made their way towards the flight-line for pre-flight checks by our Jump Master Instructor, the men walked like the quintessential cowboy, John Wayne, restricted in their super-tight harnesses. Meanwhile, the De Havilland Rapide aircraft's engines fired up drowning out the Jump Master's voice and, filtered in a line, we walked behind him towards the aircraft's tail, avoiding the spinning propellers at all costs, to make our way to the aircraft's passenger doorway. The aircraft door had been removed completely leaving a gaping open doorway for parachutists to climb into on a one-way journey to altitude. Invisible to the eye the spinning propellers blasted air so forceful it nearly knocked us off our feet as we pushed forward before clambering onto the wing and into the bare fuselage. Seated on the hard wooden floor with legs wide apart to allow room for the person in front to sit, we each held onto our own static-line with one hand, the other hand covered the reserve parachute container handle to avoid it being accidentally pulled. If the reserve handle was accidentally pulled inside the aircraft when the engines were running, the parachute could inflate in the swirling prop-blast and drag the parachutist prematurely out of the door and snag on the aircraft's tail with catastrophic consequences not only to the other parachutists, but also the pilot and the aircraft itself. In later years, on separate occasions, I witnessed reserve parachutes 'pop' in the aircraft whilst climbing to altitude causing instant reaction from everyone on board restricting the parachute from inflating and blowing out of the door.

The Rapide taxied to the end of the runway where the pilot held the brakes and applied full throttle waiting for the airflow to build up. The engine's vibrations resonated through our bodies making our teeth chatter and once the brakes released, the aircraft lunged forward from its stationary position causing the entire load to slide towards the rear of the aircraft as it gathered speed across the bumpy, grass runway. The wheels bounced on and off the ground meanwhile our backsides slammed hard on the wooden floor and only when we were airborne did we re-position into the original seating plan. At 1,000ft above the ground, the jump master snapped each person's static-line hook onto a heavy-duty cable, attached at both ends by a strong-point, and encouraged each parachutist to pull firmly confirming with thumbs up it was hooked on correctly. As number one there was no way I could possibly refuse, was there? It was effective psychology putting a female out first and an element of peer pressure presented itself both to myself and the blokes who were manifested to jump after me. I didn't want to let the girlie side down in front of the blokes and likewise, the blokes, full of bravado, didn't want to admit being the slightest bit scared either. You'd think that after watching a female jump there was no way the blokes could refuse to jump, but some did, quite spectacularly and were quite clearly out of their comfort zone. At that moment I wished I wasn't there in the aircraft, wished the weather conditions would suddenly change, wished the winds would go over the limits, wished I'd left a farewell note to my family, wished the aircraft would land again. The pilot shouted "Running in" and the jump-master moved towards the door, placed his hands on the frame and dangled outside to look under the wing checking the line of flight over the drop zone. Above the engine noise he yelled commands to the pilot, "Five left. Five left" instructing the pilot to give fine flight corrections ensuring the aircraft flew over the target area, on the wind line, to the desired exit and parachute opening point. In parachuting terms this is known as 'spotting', the fine art of dispatching parachutists so that they should drift on the correct wind-line within the wind-cone to land safely on the designated target area on the DZ. The aircraft stopped climbing and flew flat and level at 70 knots, a crucial speed so as not to blow the parachutist and the deploying parachute into the tail of the aircraft. The jump-master dangled out the door one final time to check the 'spot' then appeared again when he beckoned me forward pointing to the door. "In the door!" he shouted. "This is it! I thought, I'm going to die!" The jump master shouted a lengthy "Cuuuuuutttt" indicating the pilot cut the power. "Climb out!" he shouted. I extended my arm out of the door and grabbed hold of the diagonal strut before stepping out onto the wing. With both feet on the wing I held onto the strut for all I was worth avoiding being blown off by the air blasting from the propeller, which was spinning its ass off directly in front of me. Wearing goggles wasn't an option and with streaming eyes, my face distorted like a rubber mask, my cheeks and mouth flapped uncontrollably in the prop wash. As instructed, I turned my head to the right to look eyeball to eyeball into my jump master's face when he jabbed me sharply in the ribs and shouted "Go". The force of the jab took the air from my lungs, I released my grip, arched into a good stable position and fell away from the aircraft. I was weightless, falling and watching the aircraft fly away when instinctively, my training kicked in and I heard myself shouting "One thousand and one, one thousand and two, one thousand and three". As my parachute began lifting off my back the risers whipped past my neck and I felt for the first of many times, the searing, stinging sensation of riser burns. My C9LL parachute opened and I was in total silence. Above me blue skies, below me the lush green vastness of Salisbury Plain's patchwork carpet scattered with pockets of early morning mist. I was a different person to the person I'd been seconds earlier when standing on the wing and when I let go of the aircraft's strut the magic turned on. Nothing can describe that first thrilling feeling, the excitement, the zing of adrenaline racing in epic proportions around my body. I'd been infused with something totally overwhelming and addictive which instantly become my drug of choice and this adrenaline junky was born.

In a heartbeat, the dewy green grass rushed up to meet me until the soles of my size 10 boots (which I'd borrowed from an instructor), touched down on terra-firma. The instant feeling was one of elation but also one of disappointment for the experience was over far too quickly, not lasting nearly as long as I imagined it might. Rolling onto my front, I pulled a riser towards me hauling at the lines on one side to deflate the parachute which was beginning to drag me across the drop zone, then sprung to my feet and sprinted to its downwind side to totally collapse it. After raising my arms and waving to the drop zone controller who observed everyone's descent from the top of the tall control tower he waved back acknowledging I'd landed safely. For the next few minutes I laid down on top of my rigging lines and canopy, closed my eyes, my thumping heart beat heavily throughout my body and I mentally visualised the entire experience over and over again. To say I was bitten by the bug was a gross understatement... It was the best thing I'd ever experienced and couldn't wait to get my knees in the breeze again.

Bitten by the bug...

First Shows

03/06/1971 – Jumps 33 & 34

My first ever parachute demonstration was out of a Scout helicopter with 9 Squadron Royal Engineers (Airborne) with Major Alex Black and Sergeant Wally Clift. The demonstration was into the Royal Engineers Depot and Training camp at Southwood Barracks, Farnborough at a Passing Out Parade. With a grand total of thirty-three parachute descents, I was jumping a basic C9LL parachute and wore smoke canisters strapped to my ankles for the first time. When I landed in the middle of the small arena, the audience erupted into applause and cheers and the air buzzed with "It's a girl, it's a girl" and the audience rushed forward to request my autograph. I bashfully signed my name on anything and everything from t-shirts, hats and even some cheeks (buttocks too), arms, legs, chests and backs. After the team line-up, we packed our parachutes on the grass inside the small arena surrounded by the enthralled audience, then kitted up in preparation to jump again. The Scout helicopter had landed on the parade square next to the arena and we then boarded again to do a second jump. What a buzz it was sitting on the floor of the helicopter,

Flight-line check

dangling my legs outside the open door frame with feet placed on the skids while waving to the crowd. The pilot lifted off, hovered for a couple of minutes causing chaos to the spectators' clothing, hats flying everywhere and women trying in vain to keep their dresses blowing upwards. It was my first fifteen minutes of fame which was to be my launch pad to an incredibly exciting life. Skydiving changed my life completely, opened doors I didn't know existed and allowed me entry into an exclusive all-male military environment.

Major Alex Black had many more parachute displays scheduled for the Royal Engineer Team's forthcoming summer season and astonishingly, he invited me as a guest jumper to take part in the shows with them. I'm most thankful to him for trusting my limited experience in the sport by allowing me the opportunity to join him and his team in my early skydiving days. I owe him so much and sadly cannot thank him as in later years, Alex was killed in an air accident in Kent when the aircraft he was piloting, an EP9, crashed.

Army Championships

The British Army Parachuting Championships was my first competition, participating in the novice accuracy event. After a week of jumping out of various aircraft and mingling with the cream of the military's crop, I got to stand on the dizzying height of the medal-winners podium collecting my first ever skydiving trophy and medal, a bright, shiny gold one at that and presented by probably the British Army's most popular General, Sir Herbert John Mogg. Also competing at the Army Championships was Major Peter Schofield, the Team Commander, Parachute Regiment Freefall Team the Red Devils, accompanied by his competition team, some of whom were British National

Champions. The Red Devils were (and still are) world famous being the first British full-time military parachuting team established in 1964. During the parachuting event, I witnessed not only their parachuting skills but also their professionalism right down to the way they laid their equipment out neatly, in a line, as if on parade. They excelled in every event defending their previous years' titles winning every gong, trophy and award at the championships. After the medal and trophy presentation ceremony, I experienced my very first press call to a barrage of interest as the only female with a trophy in the all-male throng of winners and competitors. The cameras flashed like an electrical storm and should have come with a health warning or pair of sun glasses to protect my eyes. Major Schofield congratulated me on my success and nearly knocked my socks off when he told me I was a natural and could be a world champion if I applied myself to it. I couldn't believe that the Red Devils Team Commander had even spoken to me, let alone congratulate me. There is nothing more motivational than receiving praise and his congratulatory pat on the back encouraged me to achieve much greater things, and to become a world champion as he said I would. I have to say that I owe everything I am, and have done, to Major Peter Schofield and will be forever indebted to him for believing in me and giving me the opportunity in the first place. Major Schofield also had a word in my ear asking me politely to decline any more offers to perform parachute displays or casual jumping with 9 Sqn Royal Engineer's Parachute Team because he (Major Schofield) had something in the pipeline that could perhaps change my life and career. I didn't know what was in the pipeline but when I spoke with Major Alex Black he was deeply disappointed but at the same time very understanding as he obviously had an inkling that Major Schofield's agenda was to get me onto his team. The 9 Squadron Royal Engineers Team was a part-time, weekend-only team, whereas the Red Devils were full-time and the most famous worldwide, so with his blessing he wished me luck in my forthcoming career.

No sky too high!

The Parachute Regiment's Freefall Display Team

Edward Gardener

For this book, Colonel Ed Gardener kindly offered his in-depth knowledge of the Red Devil's genesis as he himself assumed the appointment of Team Commander on 1 January 1964. The following is Ed's account of the formation of the team.

"After a belated start behind France and the United States sport parachuting was, by 1963, becoming quite well established in the UK. The British Parachute Association had progressed from a collection of enthusiasts with little organisation or teeth into the recognised controlling body of the sport. While certainly not world leaders, British teams were performing very creditably at international competitions. Although successful commercial centres had yet to be established, weekend clubs were quite numerous – particularly in the South. Parachute displays were still relatively novel events but were in increasing demand at all forms of civilian and military shows. Equipment still mainly consisted of ex-US Government stock (C9/B4 main parachutes and T7a reserves) available at relatively low cost although the wealthier pundits were sporting Low Porosity TU's – the very latest in high performance, as the Para Commander was not due to appear in this country for another two years. Regrettably the two British manufacturers, Irvins and GQ, were producing little of practical value for the average parachutist and certainly not at affordable prices.

As might be expected, the Services were well to the fore in the sport. Many of the original pioneers had been RAF PJIs and a strong club was based on No 1 PTS; in addition, the school provided the official RAF Display Team (the forerunners of the Falcons) which mainly performed at RAF Air Displays. In the Army the undisputed leaders were 22 SAS; this unit had produced the entire British Team for the 1962 World Championships and regularly carried away most of the team and many of the individual trophies at national competitions. Their display team was certainly the most experienced and busiest in the Army. But although its members were able to spend much of their time parachuting, it was still only a part time team and in later years, as 22 SAS's operational commitments increased, it went into relative decline in the sport parachuting field.

In 16 Para Brigade 1, 2 and 3 PARA each had their own separate clubs. However due to frequent moves overseas and lack of continuity due to postings it was proving difficult to improve standards. 9 Para Sqn RE had an excellent team but, because of the size of the unit, it consisted of little more than its four hard core members. Most other units in the Brigade had either formed embryo clubs or at least had a handful of dedicated individuals.

Elsewhere in the Army quite a number of units and regiments were forming their own clubs, probably the most notable being the Royal Green Jackets. In order to co-ordinate all this activity the Army Parachute Association had been formed and, as a result of a generous grant from Rothmans Ltd, acquired its own Rapide aircraft. The problems faced by a handful of keen but unqualified soldiers learning to operate this aircraft is another story but, suffice to say, it was proving to be a great success. Plans were already in hand to acquire a permanent centre for the Association at Netheravon and to establish a branch in Germany – the Rhine Army Parachute Association.

I had started freefalling in 1961 while a platoon commander in 3 PARA by attending one of the first Military Freefall Courses run by No 1 PTS. With a few extra sport descents under our belts (grand total of about twenty-five!), Lance Corporal Gus Martin and I qualified as so-called BPA Instructors and, on a subsequent tour in the Gulf, ran courses for the Battalion using AAC aircraft in Aden. How we never killed or injured any of our students (or indeed ourselves as we experimented with such advanced techniques as 'relative work' with no instruction) is both a mystery and a miracle.

On our return to the UK in 1962 I was reluctantly posted to the Infantry Junior Leaders' Battalion in Oswestry as an Adventure Training Instructor, just as I was hoping to attempt SAS selection. During our Summer leave in 1963 Lance Corporal Sherdy Vatnsdal (1 PARA) and I were running freefall courses for the APA at Middle Wallop and Thruxton. During lengthy evening discussions over many pints of beer, Major John Weeks (one of the pioneers of sport parachuting in the Regiment and the first Secretary of the APA), Sherdy and I discussed the idea of forming a full time display team within Airborne Forces. We realised that there was no chance of getting such a team officially established or funded and therefore proposed that it should be largely self-financing and composed of members 'loaned' from their parent units. Because of the shortage of available talent within the Parachute Regiment we favoured the idea of a team recruited from all units within 16 Para Bde.

I wrote a short paper outlining our proposals which was sent initially to RHQ PARA. John Weeks then discussed the matter further with the new Regimental Colonel, Glyn Gilbert (who had also become the Chairman of the APA), who gave his full support to the idea. However, in order to ensure adequate control, he decided that it should be a Regimental rather than a Brigade team. In the early stages this caused considerable problems in training members to an adequate standard but in the long term proved to be a wise decision. The team today owes an enormous debt to the foresight, determination and courage of Glyn Gilbert and John Weeks who, behind the scenes, did so much to help launch and support it during its early stages.

The net result was that I was short toured at Oswestry and, on 1 January 1964, assumed the grand appointment of Commander of The Parachute Regiment Freefall Display Team; I had a small office in RHQ PARA, a lot of enthusiasm – and nothing else! On top of this I also inherited the appointment of APA Secretary from John Weeks which included the management of the Rapide aircraft.

The main problems which had to be overcome to get the team on the road were the selection and training of its members, the provision of equipment and support facilities (including parachutes, aircraft, transport and accommodation) and getting display bookings. Due to battalion commitments and manning levels it was not possible to cream off all the most experienced jumpers. 3 PARA were about to go on another one-year tour in the Gulf and could therefore only provide Sergeant Joe ('Pop') Reddick – a Second World War veteran – who, like myself, had just over one hundred freefall jumps. Next to arrive was the 1 PARA contingent who were allowed home early from their Battalion's emergency UN tour in Cyprus; this consisted of Lance Corporal Sherdy Vatnsdal (a Canadian and our greatest expert with about two hundred jumps), Privates Charlie Gowens (about one hundred jumps) and Ernie Rowberry with a slightly lower total. Finally, 2 PARA produced Second Lieutenant Simon Hill, Sergeants Bill Catt and John Hamshere, Corporals Jackie Baughan and Tom Robertson, Lance Corporals Brian David and Alec Parker, and Privates Paul Starkie and Don McNaughton. Although the largest battalion contribution they were certainly the least experienced; all had only completed a basic course and had between ten and twenty jumps each (Brian David was the least experienced and I seriously had to consider whether to keep him. Fortunately I did – he later became the National and Army Champion!) Later in the year we also acquired Sergeant Bill Scarratt on the completion of his exchange tour with the US Army at Fort Bragg where he had taken up freefalling and acquired a lot of useful experience.

To get this (even for those days) inexperienced team up to an acceptable display standard before the start of the season proved to be no mean problem. The US Army Parachute Team – the 'Golden Knights' – had kindly agreed to host us at Fort Bragg and give us several weeks' training which would have been invaluable. But unfortunately diplomatic relations with the US Government were soured when Britain sold some buses to Cuba and the invitation was cancelled! We got some excellent aircraft support from the Austers of the Para Bde Recce Flt and the Beavers of 6 Flt AAC but their available hours were limited. For the majority of training we had to hire the APA Rapide or other civilian aircraft. No funding was available and team members therefore had to dip into their own pockets to pay for their jumps. By about mid-May the level of experience had certainly improved and everyone had a minimum of about fifty jumps, but this was far from ideal. Display routines were therefore kept simple and seldom involved anything more than a close team exit from the aircraft (each man trailing smoke from a No 83 Smoke Grenade), very limited relative work and a stacked opening with the emphasis placed on a safe landing in the target area. We considered inviting some of the other more experienced parachutists from the Regiment to 'guest jump' on displays when they were available, but decided against this as we had sufficient numbers and integrating 'outsiders' who had not trained together might have increased the risks.

The solution to the personal equipment problem was, unfortunately, very simple. We established quite close links with the GQ Parachute Company thanks to the friendship and support of a member of their Board, Major 'Dumbo' Willans, a wartime member of The Parachute Regiment and a well-known test jumper and pioneer of British parachuting. We were asked to try out their new design of sport parachute called the 'Scorpion' with which they proposed to equip the team. Regrettably its performance could only be described as totally unsatisfactory and we had to turn it down. Dumbo tried to persuade the Company to produce some conventional sport parachutes for us under licence, but without success. Although we continued to get some assistance from them with minor items of equipment, we were back to square one with parachutes and all other personal kit. The inevitable result was that each member had to provide his own. It says much for the keenness and dedication of all those founder members that they were quite prepared to pay so much to carry out their official duties.

It was Glyn Gilbert who came up with the unprecedented idea that the team should acquire its own aircraft. He persuaded all the battalions, Regular and TA, to provide a total of £1000 in interest free loans – enough to buy a Rapide aircraft. Rothmans had offered a similar amount to buy one for RAPA which I, as Secretary of the APA, also had to purchase; so I had to find two suitable aircraft for sale. After a lot of hunting through contacts in the aviation world I learned that a small Middle Eastern airline were about to sell five good quality Rapides which were based in Beirut but carrying Jordanian registration. They were apparently all about to be snapped up by another interested party, however a quick telephone call to Beirut and instructions to the bank to cable out the money just secured us the best two of the bunch. Two volunteer pilots from BOAC went out to Beirut and flew them back without serious incident. However, they required a thorough overhaul before they could be awarded their British Certificates of Airworthiness, so it was about mid-June before the team had its very own jump ship in the air. We based it at Blackbushe and relied upon a superb bunch of civilian and RAF volunteer pilots to fly it. All the display fees for this first year went towards repaying the loans for its purchase but it was a very worthwhile venture which probably did much to ensure the survival and progress of the team in future years.

Although I had my office in RHQ in the now demolished Maida Barracks, there was no space available in the co-located Depot to accommodate the team. However, 1 PARA had spare buildings at their barracks at Cove and kindly agreed to administer them and provide some limited road transport. This split was not ideal but, as it turned out, worked reasonably well.

Getting bookings for displays was no great problem, thanks to the determined efforts of Major Peter Cockcraft, the Recruiting RO in RHQ. We ended up with a programme of about fifty displays for a season running from May to October. These included military events which were undertaken at no cost apart from the aircraft and civilian shows for which a fee was charged. Bad weather reduced the number of completed shows to about thirty – we imposed very strict wind speed limits for small DZs with such an inexperienced team. All were completed without injury or serious incident, although there were some cases of missed DZs with the occasional amusing result – such as the time when one parachutist undershot into a locked tennis court, much to the delight of the many press photographers present who snapped his vain attempts to escape from this very effective cage!

Colonel Ed Gardener with Red Devils, 1st January 1964

Quite unofficially the team carried out some trials into blind dropping techniques using the Beaver aircraft of 6 Flt AAC. These were at times a bit hairy but generally proved to be very successful provided that fairly accurate wind forecasts were available. These early experiments eventually led to the official military freefall trials undertaken by the team in later years.

All members of the team took part in the Army Parachute Championships, representing their parent battalions. They performed very creditably and were hard on the heels of 22 SAS. They also ran several basic courses for soldiers in the Regiment. It was a busy year filled with many problems and frustrations as well as success and much satisfaction. In the middle of it all I even got married, having changed the date twice to fit in with team commitments; most of our honeymoon was spent in a dilapidated caravan on Netheravon airfield where I was running and participating in the Army Championships. This was typical of the treatment tolerated by all the team's long suffering wives and girlfriends.

I finally left the team in the October to take over as the Adjutant of 3 PARA in Bahrain. Compared with its achievements in later years it was a small, uncertain beginning, but the Red Devils (as they were subsequently called) were at least firmly launched."

Colonel (then Lt) Ed Gardener with Prince Philip

Fully-Fledged Red Devil

For nearly a year Regimental Colonel Joe Starling corresponded with my WRAC Queen Bee in Whitehall, London, negotiating the possibility I be allowed to join the Parachute Regiment Freefall Team, The Red Devils, as a fully-fledged and full-time team member. The main purpose of the team's existence was recruiting, as jumping into show grounds around the country raised the military's and Parachute Regiment's profile. There was not a female anywhere in the world on a military team of any kind at that time. This offered the opportunity to maximise exposure and heighten awareness of not only the Parachute Regiment, but also the Women's Royal Army Corps and the then little-known sport of skydiving. The WRAC hierarchy were not impressed by his persistence and correspondence bounced back and forth when endless 'concerns' were expressed one of which, hilariously, was they didn't like the idea of me flying my parachute over the crowds at show grounds as they would be able to see up my skirt when I 'floated' overhead! In that era, it wasn't standard for women to wear trousers and even the BBC refused to allow their female staff to do so. My Queen Bee's stance caused much hilarity, rolling of eyes, head-shaking and 'I don't believe it' comments from the Parachute Regiment hierarchy. Assurances were given to my female bosses that under no circumstance would I expose my nether regions to the crowds as I 'floated' over, as my parachuting dress mode would be a protective jumpsuit and not a skirt.

Throughout 1971, I continued parachuting with the Red Devils every Monday and Wednesday afternoon at Blackbushe Airport where the team ran a part-time parachuting programme. Every weekend throughout that first summer season, from June to October, I travelled the country as ground party, laying out the drop zone in the show ground arena, setting up the ground-to-air communication in the form of a fluorescent cross and igniting the smoke flares to give visual wind direction to the team members approaching the arena from under their parachutes. The crowd always assume that the cross in the middle of the arena is a target for the parachutists to land on and cheer loudly when the parachutists land on or close to it, but back in the day, the cross was the only ground-to-air communication as we didn't have radios then. Team members however, always aimed to land on the cross with enthusiastic in-team competition and whoever landed furthest from the cross was slated with good humoured banter, the penalty of 'getting the brews or beers in'. Flying over the show ground, the jumpers on board the aircraft observed the fluorescent panels set out in either

Red Team

an I, X, T or L configuration in the middle or to the side of the arena. The 'I' indicated to the jumpers in the aircraft that the DZ party was aware of the aircraft's presence. The 'T' configuration meant the parachutists should hold off and circle above the arena at jump altitude (or air clearance altitude) due to perhaps an over-running show in the arena, be it brass bands, animals of some sort, show-jumping horses and fences, dogs or motor-bikes etc. As soon as the 'T' configuration changed to a cross or 'X' it was our 'clear to drop' instruction and the show ground was ready for us to parachute into. If the panel configuration was an 'L' it meant that the show organiser himself or ground party had cancelled the parachute drop due to perhaps extremely high winds or some other drop zone hazardous situation or incident.

On parade

Aldershot Army Show 1971

With cutaway canopy

With a lot of persuasion, my WRAC Queen Bees agreed to let me join the team on a full-time basis and Major Schofield courteously wrote to my parents advising them I would be joining The Parachute Regiment Freefall Team, The Red Devils as a full-time member of an all-male team, giving assurance that the other 29 male members of the team would look after me. My Mam and Dad were absolutely over the moon, chuffed to bits with delight and so proud of me. What an honour!

From the first day I set foot into the Team Room a frenzy of press activity ensued, and I became the face of the military, making regular appearances on TV news, chat shows, children's programmes, newspapers and radio stations, not only in the UK but across the globe. Prior to actually 'going live' to the public, I'd been briefed by Major Schofield who told me I was in an incredibly unique place in history and advising that I take it all in my stride, not let the Army down or bring the Parachute Regiment into disrepute. Being interviewed by the press was something I'd have to get used to doing and I should endeavour to do it professionally, as an ambassador of the military and also the sport. Over the years I learned to handle the most invasive of press interviewers who instead of asking for information about skydiving or life on the team, tried to get a juicy story out of me. Bizarrely, some reporters were only interested in knowing if I had seen the men on the team naked, asking did they undress in front of me. I divulged nothing to the press that they could distort or write shock,

From : Team Commander

The RED DEVILS

Ref: FFT 3A/72

The Parachute Regiment
Free Fall Team,

Browning Barracks,
ALDERSHOT,
Hants.

Tel: Aldershot 24431 ext. 2446

THE PARACHUTE REGIMENT FREEFALL TEAM
THE RED DEVILS 1972

1. During 1971 over 4 million spectators have already been entertained by the Parachute Regiments famous Freefall Team, The Red Devils. The organisers of the many shows attended by the Team this season know how the crowds enjoy our thrilling display of individual and Team parachuting skills using up to three different types of parachute with their many and varied characteristics.

2. For those organisations who have not been entertained by the spectacle of the Team leaving an aircraft at heights of up to 11,000 feet, freefalling to 2,000 feet before opening their parachutes and then making precision landings may we highlight some of the coming years additional attractions.

3. Especially for the children (and press) we will be introducing 'Red Fred', our parachuting Gorilla, and to cater for womans lib (and the press again) we hope to add a touch of glamour in the very femenine form of Lcpl Jackie Smith, WRAC, The British Novice Champion - our first lady team member.

4. Though our season continues well into October, we have now started planning for 1972, for which we already have a considerable number of bookings. In order that YOU the organiser will not be dissapointed by not having the best parachute display Team available for your show may we advise you to contact us as soon as possible - certainly before mid November.

5. A phone call now would secure a tentative booking, an estimate of cost and despatch of booking forms etc.

(B.S. SCHOFIELD)
Major,
Team Commander

Press Release 1972

horror sordid stories to sell their newspapers. Imagine the field day they'd have had if I told them I could recognise any of my team mates from 1000 metres, stark bollock naked. I knew every inch of their bodies right down to their hairy bum holes which they took great pleasure in exposing when mooning. And then there was the pressed ham version of mooning when a hairy arse was pressed against glass, be it an office or vehicle window where, if they applied lots of pressure, their meat and two veg squished on the glass too. On one particular unguarded moment Major Schofield made a sarcastic comment which he thought was out of earshot of a reporter and said "Jackie drinks pints of Guinness, smokes a pipe and swears like a trooper". The reporter actually printed those words in the national press and the following day, my army Queen Bee's advisories came straight down on me like a ton of bricks wanting to know what on earth I was doing on the team. I admit to drinking the pints of Guinness however, but have never smoked a pipe or felt the need to swear apart from when missing the disc because of bad foot placement on an accuracy jump. It's a common expression amongst accuracy jumpers to say 'shit' when missing the target and over the years attending international competitions I've become multilingual expressing frustration instead with 'merde', 'scheisse', or the American double syllable word 'shiyett'.

Packing my parachute

The Red Devils had been in existence for nearly ten years as a world famous, highly reputable and successful all-male military team and the last thing the military hierarchy and Major Schofield wanted was for me to attract adverse publicity as I was in full glare of the world's media. Major Schofield emphasised in no uncertain terms that on joining the team I would receive no concessions for being female and should get used to everything that went on in the team's all-male environment, be it their nakedness, bathroom humour or choice language and reminding me that it was me who was joining the team and not the team joining me. I was a lone female in the maroon machine that is the elite Parachute Regiment and no way was I about to jeopardise the fantastic opportunity because even at that early stage in my skydiving career, I was incredibly driven, with aspirations of becoming a World Champion. I was all too aware that being a full-time member of the Team was the perfect platform to launch and achieve my ambitions, where with expert colleagues offering guidance, coaching and the use of most up-to-date equipment, I really was in the best company to achieve my goal. I was living the dream!

My absolute dream lifestyle could easily have turned into a nightmare on that awful day, 22nd February 1972, when a bomb went off at 16 Para Brigade Officers Mess, Aldershot. During the early 1970s, military personnel became extremely vigilant regarding personal security as the troubles in Northern Ireland had kicked off. The Parachute Regiment and therefore the Red Devils Parachute Team, became potential targets for retaliation from the IRA terrorist organisation.

That fine February morning, after visiting the military dentist on Knolly's Road, I cycled the route to the team offices, cutting through Pennefather's Road passing close by to 16 Parachute Brigade Officers' Mess. No longer than a minute later I arrived at the Team room office, leaned my bike against the wall and 'boom!', an almighty explosion shook the building and in slow motion the glass windows bulged outwards like a bubble before bursting, then smashed to smithereens, the force sprayed glass shards in all directions inside of the building. For a minute or so there was a deathly silence in the air and from the skies, snow appeared to be falling. To this day, I don't know if it was snow or debris dust. Every window in the Team offices, education centre and the close-by Normandy Barracks Naafi, gymnasium and band room was smashed, the glass scattered all around. It was about fifteen minutes after noon and the explosion was caused by a huge bomb which had been planted in a car and parked at the car park at 16 Parachute Brigade Headquarters Officer's Mess entrance, the very car park I'd cycled past just a minute or so prior to it detonating.

Tragically, the explosion took the lives of five female kitchen staff, Thelma Bosley, a single mum raising three young boys (her eldest son aged 22 was serving with the Parachute Regiment); Margaret Grant, a mother of three children and wife of ex-Parachute Regiment soldier; Joan Lunn, a mother of three; Jill Mansfield, a mother of one; Sheri Munton; the military gardener John Hasler and Captain Gerry Weston MBE, the military padre and Roman Catholic Priest. Such was the size of the bomb the blast was felt a mile away in the Aldershot town centre. In a state of shock, I walked from the team room towards the plumes of smoke and demolished Officer's Mess. It was a scene of total devastation where soldiers and emergency services were rushing around helping the injured and digging through the debris with their bare hands. That Tuesday was the saddest of days and will be etched forever in the minds of those who were there when terrorism arrived on Aldershot's doorstep.

A brief history of Major Peter Schofield

As a young lad, Peter joined the Royal Navy in 1959 and decided to transfer to the Army, completed P Company and on his 7th jump broke his ankle, landing straight down, and in his words, 'like a fucking tent peg'. To add insult to injury when the ambulance arrived on the DZ, they ran over his hand and broke his fingers. He later completed the military jumps to attain his airborne wings and joined the Parachute Regiment, his Battalion was the 2nd Battalion which he affectionately called 'My Battalion'.

AERIAL COMMENTARY

In addition to the normal ground based commentary, the RED DEVILS can now give a "second-by-second" account of their demonstrations, from the aircraft, in free fall, and from under the canopy, right up to the time of landing. Through a good Public Address system the airborne commentary is clearly audible to all spectators. It is made possible by a miniature FM transmitter working in conjunction with a helmet-mounted boom microphone and a special antenna worn by one of the parachutists, usually the Team Commander. The transmission is picked up by a miniature transistorised receiver, and broadcast through the Public Address system. This thrilling innovation, pioneered by the RED DEVILS, has taken three years to perfect and enables spectators to hear clearly for the first time the voice of a man falling earthwards at speeds of up to 180 miles per hour. After the "crack" of his parachute opening, they enjoy a detailed first-hand account and explanation of the parachutist's every manoeuvre as he guides himself into the arena. This radio microphone system has been custom built for the RED DEVILS by Lustraphone Ltd., of London, England.

Major Schofield

In 1963, sport parachuting was in its infancy and most units within the Airborne Forces had formed small sport parachute freefall clubs and although parachute displays were relatively novel events, it was considered a potential recruiting platform at both military and civilian shows. Some teams emerging in Aldershot at the same time as The Red Devils were 7 Royal Horse Artillery (Black Knights), 9Sqn (Para) Royal Engineers, Silver Stars (Royal Corps of Transport), Royal Army Ordnance Corps Team and many individual sport parachutists from other airborne units, 216 Para Royal Signals, 1 Parachute Logistic Regiment, 63 Squadron (Para) RCT and airborne REME.

Major Schofield joined Junior Parachute Company at Depot Para a couple of years later and did his first sport parachute jump at Netheravon in March/April 1966 under the watchful eye of highly experienced sport parachutists who had helped form the Parachute Regiment's Display Team, The Red Devils. Members of the team were Sgt Sherdy Vatnsdal, Sgt Bill Scarratt who was the 1966 British National Parachuting Champion and Sgt Bill Catt.

In 1967, Major Peter Kingston was Team Commander of the Red Devils and he invited Major Schofield to join the team for a parachute training expedition to Pau, France and achieved 41 jumps in two weeks which was considered a real achievement at the time. On their return to the UK, the team wiped the board at the Army Parachute Championships winning every medal there was to be competed for, with Major Schofield winning the novices event. In July 1968 the team set a record for doing military parachuting from 25,000ft at night and also did group cloud penetration jumps, which had never been trialled before and took part in HALO jumps into the Mull of Kintyre from Argosy aircraft.

Major Schofield assumed the role of Team Commander the following year and arranged a training camp in the USA. The team travelled to New Jersey in 1969 and met Steve Snyder who took Major Schofield to a secret drop zone where he saw the Nicolaides Foils and Para-Planes being jumped. Steve was test jumping the Irvin Delta II Para Wing, a triangular parachute which was a new innovation. The suspension lines were held together where they joined the canopy with a huge Velcro strap and when the canopy began to deploy it developed dreadful opening characteristics, usually resulting in it being cut away. There were a number of injuries due to vicious openings which had no reliability whatsoever and on one occasion when the parachute opened particularly hard, the whites of Dick Morgan's eyes turned completely bloodshot red. Regardless of the inconsistency of successful openings, Major Schofield ordered four for the team and when they arrived at Orange DZ, they were all rigged incorrectly with wrong line lengths. Steve Snyder sent new line sets to the hotel at Lakewood where the team were staying and they changed the lines in the hotel lobby, while hotel guests looked on in horror.

The Team had some interesting company in Lakewood when the local Mafia turned up on the DZ challenging an accuracy competition using beer-mats as targets. Those jumping Para Commanders planted the beer mat, apart that is, from Brian David (who was British National Champion at the time) who landed with his heels either side of it. It turned out Brian had been bribed to lose the competition in a Mafia betting plot and came away with a handful of big number dollars and a boozy night followed where they made firm friends with their Mafia punters. Later in the week while driving the DZ Inn-keeper's car, Jack Fowler hit another vehicle being driven by an elderly lady when she pulled out in front of him. It was clearly the elderly lady's fault, but Jack was a stranger in town therefore was arrested immediately and put in jail. Through the labyrinth of communications, word reached the Mafia that a member of the

Red Devils, Jack, was in jail and through their renown persuasive negotiating skills, made the local Magistrate an offer he couldn't refuse. Jack was immediately released with no further charges and so relieved to be freed, bought the beers for being the first Red Devil to spend a night in a USA slammer.

Earlier, in 1967, the Golden Knights Gene-Paul Thacker and Bob McDermott visited the UK after competing at the World Championships and the team forged lasting friendships with them. Later that year the team were invited by the United States Army Parachute Team, The Golden Knights, to their training facility in Fort Bragg, North Carolina for a training camp and took part in some parachute displays with the USA Team whilst there. One of the parachute displays was into Fairmont Park in Philadelphia where Major Schofield did the first ever Aerial Commentary in the world and from there the team were invited to jump into the United States Air Force Thunderbird Team reunion. It would have been rude not to accept the invite to the Thunderbirds evening celebration and I understand the heavy night of drinking continued into the early hours of the following day. For two days afterwards, the team were incapacitated by hangovers and not surprisingly, didn't turn up for parachute training. Major Schofield said the hangover was the worst he had ever suffered; it was so bad he reckoned it would have killed a crap hat (non-airborne soldier).

In May 1970, Major Schofield visited the Notre Dame University in Indiana with Steve Snyder and Dick Morgan (ex-Golden Knight) where they ran a programme flying square parachutes and later that year the team took the first delivery of Foil Parachutes and Para-Planes outside the USA. The canopies caused quite a lot of controversy and the civilian governing bodies in the United Kingdom (British Parachute Association) and certain individuals didn't like the new innovation. The issue of jumping them became a running battle between the team and the BPA who tried to ban their use. Also, the team started using quick release smoke brackets after a Golden Knight was killed when his main parachute entangled with the smoke bracket. He deployed his reserve parachute and that too caught onto the smoke bracket. The BPA didn't like the new innovation and again objected to the team using a quick release. Needless to say, the team won the battle with the BPA and performed the very first parachute displays in the UK using the Delta II Para Wing and rectangular parachutes (Para-Plane), using the smoke bracket with quick release system. Major Schofield decided to call it a day as a member of the BPA council as it was riddled with politics and his progressive and innovative drive caused a lot of unhappiness with the older BPA members. Major Schofield gave his all in the sport and the Red Devils were ahead in all aspects of training and equipment. The UK would have caught up eventually in terms of innovation, but Major Schofield's forwarding thinking brought about change so much quicker. He gave his ultimate best for the Red Devils team and in doing so, for the rest of the skydivers in Britain.

The Red Devils ran two De Havilland Rapide aircraft in parallel (G-AKIF and G-AGTM, the latter named Valkerie) at Blackbushe airport and both were hangered and serviced at Farnborough RAE. In the winter of 1970, during a routine service of the Rapide's wings, it was noted that the shoelace system (canvas cover) was undone and the frame beneath was rotten. It was the end of the road for the Tango Mike as a jump aircraft for the team, but I'm happy to say that she is still flying today.

Peter Cadbury, a descendant of the Quaker chocolate-making dynasty, was selling off his Britten Norman piston Islander and Major Schofield offered the Rapide to Rothmans (a British tobacco company) for £8,000 and hoped it would be enough to put down as a deposit for the Islander. After much negotiation, Rothmans bought the Rapide for the full asking price and The Red Devils bought G-AXDH for £45,000. The Daily Express newspaper saw the team as an advertising platform and came up with a £20,000 sponsorship deal. The actual deposit put down on the Islander was £25,000, the remaining £20,000 was paid back over a period of five years with payments of £850 per month for the duration. The remaining £3,000 was spent on painting the aircraft (Monaco Red) and fitting it with de-icing boots (which was done at Heathrow airport). The Team were (and still are) completely self-supporting with team members on loan from the 3 Parachute Battalions. There was no military support at all, no military vehicles, fuel or equipment and every penny made doing parachute displays went into the team's coffers to support the aircraft's upkeep. For the following few years, the team lived hand-to-mouth financially and fortunately the busy show seasons brought in enough revenue to keep the team's account afloat.

On 28th May 1970, The Red Devils jumped into the Royal Ulster Show and Major Schofield made the decision to jump the Delta II Para Wing while wearing a radio microphone. He found himself approaching the arena in close airspace next to Stu Cook and his intended gentle turn away resulted in familiar reverse control of his canopy and he flew off in the opposite direction to where he wanted to fly, narrowly missing Stu in mid-air and resulted in a heavy and awkward landing. He broke his ankle and gave the crowd an impromptu swearing and cursing commentary via his radio microphone over the public announcement system.

1970 saw the team invited to jump into what must be considered their hairiest demo at the Formula 1 Grand Prix at the Principality of Monaco for the Young Presidents Association (YPO). The YPO was an organisation for millionaires who met every few months for seminars keeping abreast of businesses and commerce around the world. The race route is different these days and what is now a tunnel, was then a clay pigeon shoot, a 30 metre diameter arena sitting next to mountainous rocks with a 50ft sheer cliff-face to the sea. Major Schofield and Stu Cooke were jumping Para-Plane canopies, Sooty Standring was on the cutaway (using a Para-Commander as his main), the rest were on Para-Commanders. Stu Cooke jumped with an 18" square box containing a beautiful orchid for Princess Grace of Monaco for which team rigger, Sergeant Albert Hooker, had made a harness. Stu actually cried with laughter in freefall attempting to control his stability as the box skidded him across the sky. Putting their accuracy skills to the extreme test, everyone landed safely in the small circle and the cutaway canopy landed on top of the VIP crowd of millionaires. They were all too occupied sipping champagne and eating caviar to notice the canopy land amongst them and also because they were all merrily singing happy birthday to Al Young who landed last, standing up in the middle of the cross. There was only one injury when Stu took a huge chunk out of his knee when landing and when Princess Grace was introduced to the team on the line-up she commented to Stu, "Your technical excellence is only exceeded by your ability to hide pain!"

The following year, WO2 Ted Lewington returned from his tour with 3 Para in Malta to take over the role as Team Sergeant Major from Jersey Raibit.

Team Photo Shoot

1970s

Throughout the 1970s we performed hundreds of parachute displays annually into show grounds, fields and arenas located throughout the UK which brought much needed revenue into the Team's purse. On my second year on the team, a total of 239 firm show bookings were confirmed as early as February that same year with another 70 or so further late bookings made as last minute additions. These shows were separate from the military shows we were obliged to jump into, along with every Passing Out Parade into Depot the Parachute Regiment's Browning Barracks. Extra income was also ploughed into the team's funds by operating regular parachuting courses for the general public, initially at Blackbushe airport, where we ran one-jump static-line courses for civilians. In 1972 Major Schofield was successful in getting Queens Avenue cleared for a parachute operation and from then on, all interested military personnel and civilians were trained there, on the Team's drop zone. The team fund provided for the essential parachuting equipment and maintenance and also team training raising the standards of new and regular team members up to the highly skilled parachutists they were (and still are) required to maintain highly professional expertise.

During the week when the team were not training on Queens Avenue, I was employed in the team office with the Team Sergeant Major Ted Lewington, CSgt Lawrie Casey, Sgt Dave Sands and Team Clerk, Sgt Jim Petherbridge, administering and organising the day-to-day tasks dealing with show bookings and lengthy planning preparation organising the logistics of each and every parachute display. We didn't have an official clerk so I carried out a lot of the team admin, typing letters, filing, answering the telephone, arranging flight planning and air clearance for shows, applying for Notice to Airmen (NOTAMs) with the Civilian Aviation Authority, DZ Recces, obtaining land-owner's permission to parachute onto his land, notification to police 'local-to-each-show ground', aircraft hire and any other special requirements, for instance, obtaining a specific flag or rugby ball to jump into a big match at Wembley or Murrayfield. Other 'day jobs' within the Team environment ranged from storeman (Sgt Joe Greig), cameraman and film editor, Sgt Steve Slater and rigger (repairing and packing parachutes) Sgt Albert Hooker BEM. Albert serviced and maintained not only the Red Devil's equipment but every sport parachutist in the military in Aldershot at the time. He qualified as a US Army Parachute Rigger in 1964 and as a FAA Master Rigger in 1970 and his wealth of experience and knowledge of advanced parachutes was second to none. In 1956 Albert took part in the airborne assault on Suez and despite losing a leg in an accident in 1964, continued to parachute with the team during training sessions. Albert was everyone's friend, especially when they wanted parachutes repaired or reserves packed and his skills saved a lot of lives who lived to tell their tale. Joe Greig, the team's expert skydiver, commentator and storeman was responsible for over 1200 individual items of team equipment ranging from parachutes to the team's Britten Norman Islander and its attendant book-keeping.

When we weren't on the road, Major Schofield wasn't allowed into the Team Room before 9am under strict orders from Sgt Major Ted Lewington. Some thought this was to give Major Schofield a well-earned lie-in which he took advantage of as he enjoyed reading the Daily Telegraph to keep in touch with the world. Ted, in Sgt Major fashion however, ordered a Scale A Parade for the rest of us each morning when he used the officer-free couple of hours to knock us into shape, dish out jobs and try to make our lives as miserable as possible. He took no prisoners and didn't have a fuse, he just went 'BANG' and anyone who crossed his path when he was in a bad mood stood the chance of a serious nose-to-nose bollocking. On more than one occasion, I saw him throw a full cup of coffee or typewriter across the office aimed at anyone who dared look at him or simply walk past his office door. Away from the responsibility of rank and privilege and on the level playing fields of skydiving and in the bars drinking each other under the table, Ted however, was everyone's friend. By the time Major Schofield breezed into the office each day, the entire team area was cleaned and tidied, the floors bulled to a high shine and the vehicles washed, polished and serviced, as was the aircraft in preparation for the day ahead. We were never caught out at short-notice if a visitor or high ranking military personnel, press, TV and Radio dropped by unexpectedly.

Other daily jobs were undertaken by all team members, stores management, daily equipment maintenance and repair and importantly polishing the team's championships silverware which was proudly displayed on full show at the building entrance. A job I particularly enjoyed was replying to the abundance of fan mail the team received and sending out memorabilia and signed photographs. Any down time was usually on a Tuesday, if we were allowed, when we each took care of personal admin, banking, personal laundry and team uniform as in jumpsuits, tracksuits etc as the rest of the week and weekends, we were full on with training and preparation for the weekends 'show-time' around the country.

One of my most frequent callers on the team telephone was the Regimental Sergeant Major, Nobby Arnold. Be afraid; be very afraid! I saw fully-grown men and other senior ranks hiding behind walls avoiding any contact with him for fear of what he might do or say. Nobby had risen through the military ranks to his god-like status earning him the prerogative to inflict ridicule and fear on anyone who crossed his path. He was a force to be reckoned with, the most respected and scariest Sergeant Major in the Parachute Regiment if not in whole of the British military. Rumour had it he once dropped his highly polished pace-stick on the sacred ground that was his parade square and instructed the regimental police to arrest it and place it in a prison cell. He also put a soldier in the prison cell for having a spider on his bed, charging him with keeping livestock without permission. I'd had the misfortune of an earlier encounter with him when crossing his path after visiting Jean in the paymaster's office at Browning Barracks. Nobby appeared from nowhere, his face in front of mine, our noses millimetres from touching. His deep nasal voice boomed, "Do you like my nose?" Quaking in my shoes I stood to attention and replied meekly, "Yes sir! It's a lovely nose Sir!" He walked around me as if on parade inspection, his eyes looking me up and down from head to foot and eventually his face arrived directly in front of mine again. He told me he needed an errand running and that I should go to Browning Barracks stores and collect an item for him, then return with it to the Pay Office. Fearing for my very existence I raced to the stores, pushed open the swing doors and told the store-man that Nobby had sent me for a 'short weight'. As soon as those words crossed my lips it dawned on me what I'd just asked for... a short wait, and Nobby had well and truly stitched me up. Blushing with embarrassment for asking such a stupid question I burst out laughing, as did the store-man, who, with not an iota of compassion, fell about in hysterics belly laughing for a good ten minutes before disappearing behind a stack of blankets and bedding where he continued laughing uncontrollably. After being so stupid I didn't dare go back to the Pay Office to see Nobby and instead ran out of Browning Barracks across Montgomery Square, returning to the team room as fast as my legs would carry me.

Out of breath, I ran into the Team Room office where the telephone was ringing so I rushed to pick up the receiver and answered in precise military fashion, "Parachute Regiment Freefall Team, Corporal Smith speaking, Sir!" I heard the voice on the other end of the line and nearly died right there and then. It was Nobby! In his loud nasal tone, he told me to confirm who I was again, "Is that Corporal Smith of the Parachute Regiment Freefall Team?" So scared I do believe I tinkled in my pants, I replied, "Yes, Sir! Corporal Smith speaking, Sir!" Nobby's reply was so loud I held the handset at arm's length so that everyone else around me could also hear. "Corporal Smith!" he shouted. "I hope you are standing to attention while you are talking to me". "Yes Sergeant Major!"

I answered sharply, "I am standing to attention, Sir". "Corporal Smith" he said, "during your tour on the Red Devils Parachute Team, I am ordering you to keep your feet and knees together at all times, even when you are NOT parachuting!" and at that he put the phone down. Nobby called the team office regularly throughout my time on the team and every time I answered, he took me through the exact same conversation again. If it was some other team member who answered the phone, he told them to pass on the message not to forget to keep my feet and knees together.

My first ever overseas trip was with the Team in March 1972 to the Joint Service Parachute Centre at Bad Lippspringe, Germany, shortly after I joined as a full time member. The road party travelled en masse in the Bedford sponsored team vehicles, meanwhile the Team Commander Major Schofield and Sergeant Major Ted Lewington along with a chosen few, flew in the Team's Britten Norman Islander aircraft, G-AXDH for a three-week parachute training camp. For as long as the days were light, from dawn to dusk, we jumped and repacked our parachutes, until the final lift of the day took off on the sunset load.

The Team's training objective in Germany's milder climate was to improve our personal in-air skydiving skills and also practice accuracy landings into either the pea-gravel area or into a taped-off arena measuring 75 x 75ft. It was a requirement to land consistently within these areas in order to be 'signed off' and cleared to jump into displays and shows in the UK, and in doing so, we complied with Sport Parachuting's governing body, the British Parachute Association's rules and regulations. At the end of the three-week training camp the qualifying test for the new team members was to jump into our first Red Devil's official show into Sennelager Training Centre for the Camp Commandant

Red Devils line up in Germany

Team line up

and military personnel's families' day. At the pre-jump briefing we were advised that the arena was not a grassy field similar to that we had trained and jumped onto during the previous weeks, but was in fact a small, concrete parade square in the centre of a busy military camp. The hazards to us parachutists were the flag-posts, soldiers' accommodation blocks, office blocks and buildings, electricity cables, tall 'anti-parachutist' trees and metal fences topped with curly razor wire. We kitted up with our parachute equipment and smoke canisters strapped to our ankles, emplaned and took off. This was to be the acid test! Everything we had learned in training we had to put into practice on a live demo.

With a racing heart, dry mouth, trembling hands and an overwhelming urge to throw up, the aircraft climbed to altitude where we threw a wind drift indicator at 2,000ft above the parade square. Stu pointed out the exit and opening point and I watched him with intent awaiting his signal for me to move to the open door and exit. I wasn't afraid of jumping but my biggest fear by far was letting the Team down, making a hash of landing in the arena and ruining the team's reputation. I didn't want to give anyone the opportunity to give lip service to the Paras for having a girl on the team. I also didn't want to jeopardise my future career on the team either, so failure to land in that arena was not an option. I simply had to stay focussed, switch on, read the upper winds, be aware of the other parachutes around me and fly the parachute correctly.

Jumping with a higher performance round parachute, a French Papillon, I negotiated the wind, flew within the confines of an imaginary wind-cone and faced into wind to approach my flight line towards the arena. It was a strange feeling flying over the hundreds of faces looking skywards towards me, but I couldn't let their eyes distract me from focussing on where I was going to land. With tippy-toe softness, my feet touched down gently in the centre of the cross in the middle of the tarmacked parade square and it was as if my landing flipped a switch from silence to deafening applause and cheering. In the midst of the audience's gaze, I fumbled unsuccessfully with trembling hands to undo my helmet chin strap, so gave up and attempted to loosen my harness leg straps to remove my parachute assembly. Thankfully Sgt Stu Cook came to my rescue and loosened all my equipment for me to step out of it. Sooty Standring had been selected to perform the cutaway on the show. The cutaway was the most spectacular manoeuvre performed by the team which was awe inspiring for the crowds below. Sooty exited the aircraft wearing three parachutes and at approximately 4,500ft opened the first parachute, an old, round canopy. Releasing both Capewell covers, he hooked an arm through one set of risers and pulled the ring to cutaway that same side. The canopy remained inflated and stable at this point. He then pulled the Capewell ring on the other set of risers which immediately streamed the parachute causing him to go back into freefall where he fell for two thousand feet holding onto the streaming parachute, the orange smoke spewing from the canister on his ankle emphasised the freefall speed as he fell. The crowds screamed with horror thinking one of the Red Devils was going to go in! At 2,000ft, he let go of the streaming canopy and deployed his main parachute and while he steered towards the arena for landing, the cutaway canopy usually also landed in the arena due to the highly skilled judgement of getting out of the aircraft in the correct place. It was a fine art cutting a canopy away and being in the correct place upwind of the arena to ensure it landed in it, and on that and every occasion I saw the cutaway being demonstrated, the cutaway canopy always landed in the arena! Free of my harness and helmet I ran towards the rest of the team who were forming a team line-up in front of the audience and dignitaries. Standing 'at-ease' the Team Leader called us to "Team!, Team-Shun" when we came sharply to attention awaiting introduction to the Camp Commandant and other VIPs. I was the shortest team member so was at the end of the line but my 5'4" height suddenly felt ten feet tall. I was so incredibly proud. The Camp Commandant offered me his hand and in an over-enthusiastic handshake, crushed my knuckles making my smile stretch into a polite, wide-mouthed wince. The handshake lingered for a few minutes while he repeatedly said, "Well done! Well done! Amazing! Well done!" and I never thought he would let go. The finale to the show was for the Team Leader to dismiss us. He shouted loudly, "Team! Faaaaaaaaaaall out!" We turned sharply in unison to the right, slammed in our left foot to stand to attention, raised our right hands to

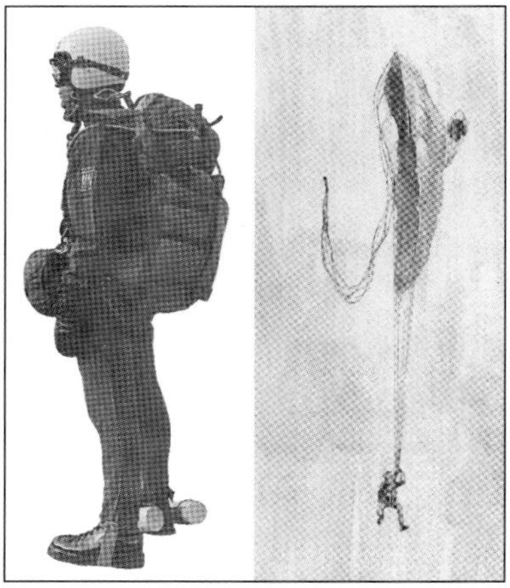
The cutaway rig

salute before stepping forward into an energetic sprint towards our personal equipment. In the instant we fell out from the line-up the audience mobbed me for autographs, everyone asking questions or wanting to shake my hand remarking that I was a girl. Eventually, I broke free and escaped the enthusiastic crowd and returned to join the rest of the team who had been waiting patiently in the team vehicles for me to join them. Sergeant Bob Harman jokingly said that the rest of the team were only there to make up the numbers as everyone was interested in the girl on the team. Sgt Major Lewington asked, "Was that your first official demo with the Red Devils?" then told me to get my arse into gear as he couldn't wait any longer to taste the 'first' of the many cases of beer I had to get in.

Downwind Accuracy Landing

In good skydiving tradition celebrating every 'first' is a rite of passage and as you can imagine, most of my wages during my first year on the team was spent on 'first' cases of beer. My firsts included first trip overseas; first jump in Germany; first kiss pass in freefall; first birthday abroad; first birthday on the team; first time I landed on the airfield; first time I went to sleep abroad; first time I woke up abroad; first shower in Germany; first time I ordered Pommes-frites from the bratwurst snack-bar; first time I packed my parachute abroad and they even tried to make me buy a case of beer for the first time I went to the toilet in Germany. My proudest 'case of beer' however, was celebrating being the first female member on The Parachute Regiment's Freefall Team, The Red Devils – how absolutely amazing a feeling that was, and yes, I got hammered, steaming drunk celebrating the occasion.

With Team training completed and successful training jumps accomplished every new team member was 'signed off' to perform parachute displays and the time came to pack our bags and return to our home base in Aldershot. The forthcoming demonstration season was approaching and with nearly three hundred parachute displays booked in for the summer season, we certainly had our work cut out. It was Show Time!

Fetch me my Brown Trousers

In early April 1972, I participated at my first 'live' parachute display in the UK as a full-time team member. The show ground was in Swansea where we were to perform two shows a day, an early and a late display on both Saturday and Sunday at 12noon and 4pm. The arena was in a field not far from Mumbles Harbour and as part of the pre-show-organisation, two lifeboats had been booked to patrol the waters in the eventuality of any of us landing in the sea. The first show of the day was scheduled for midday and we flew over the arena throwing the wind drift indicators (WDIs) directly over the arena at 2000ft to assess the wind direction and strength. For my non-skydiver readers, the 'WDIs' are home-made and measure 22ft long, 12 inches wide and made out of brightly coloured, red and yellow crepe paper making them visible as they drift to earth to the jumpers inside the aircraft. The 'WDIs' have a small weight, usually plasticine, rolled into the bottom to make them fall to the ground at the same rate of descent as a person underneath a round, unmodified parachute giving an indication of the strength and direction of the wind.

On the first show of the day, the WDIs drifted and landed quite a significant distance from where they were thrown over the arena, deeming the winds too strong and way over the safety limits. We cancelled the show from the aircraft then the pilot flew a low swooping pass over the show ground arena tipping his wing, allowing us to wave to the disappointed crowds below and at the same time a team member dangled a leg out the door with his ignited smoke grenade leaving a spectacular orange trail across the skies behind us. As the aircraft came into land at Swansea Airport, I should have kept my big mouth shut but made the mistake of mentioning to Joe Grieg that I'd never landed in an aircraft before. He immediately blurted out to the rest of the team, "Jackie has to get a case of beers in for her first landing in an aircraft!"

As the day unfolded, landing in the aircraft for the first time wasn't to be the only new experience that day. The later show into the same show ground was not scheduled until 4pm and hanging around airfields came with the boredom of swinging our legs, playing card games and practising keepy-uppie football while some drank the vending machine dry of its tea and coffee. As 3.30pm approached we kitted up and boarded the aircraft again in preparation for the next show. The winds were still blowing briskly but the WDI on this occasion didn't travel 'quite' so far as earlier in the day. Flying around, we all voted on whether or not to jump and a unanimous decision was made. It was a goer! We were jumping! The fluorescent orange cross in the middle of the arena was in the X configuration when we flew overhead indicating 'clear to drop' and the show ground below was ready to receive us. "Running in" shouted the pilot and he flew the aircraft in a straight line directly over where the WDI had landed, overhead the arena and continued into wind until we approached our exit point. I was to exit first with my team mate, Sgt Steve Slater, and as I dived through the door I pulled the smoke bomb ignitor cord and felt the top of my parachute pack hit hard against the door frame throwing me unstable into the slipstream. Steve and I made contact as we had planned and intentionally spun in circles while the trailing orange smoke spewed from the pyrotechnics strapped to our ankles. I gave him a quick kiss-pass then we turned 180 degrees away from other, straightened our legs and arms and tracked, creating space between us to open up our parachutes. The needle on my altimeter approached opening altitude so I grasped the ripcord, removed it from its retaining pocket on the harness and pulled hard to release the metal pins from the parachute pack on my back. The ripcord was jammed in place and wouldn't budge so I placed both hands on the handle applying all my strength, but to no avail. The ripcord pins remained firmly in the grommets and the parachute pack stayed closed. I didn't know it at the time but the parachute pack top metal plate and first ripcord pin had bent to a 180-degree angle after jarring into the aircraft door on exit, making it impossible for the pins to release. Falling at a speed of 120 miles an hour the seascape below was getting closer and closer and without further hesitation I executed my well-practised emergency drills and pulled the chest-mounted reserve metal handle to deploy my emergency parachute. The reserve parachute was mounted on the front of my parachute harness assembly and as it began to deploy the drag from the canopy and risers pulled me from my face-to-earth freefall position into a standing up position while still falling to earth. Visibility of the reserve parachute deploying was obscured from view by pungent, orange smoke trailing up the length of my body filling my nostrils and mouth but that was the least of my problems. The reserve parachute opened viciously with a bang, my vision went blurry and I felt light-headed. I glanced upwards and saw the reserve canopy was inside out, inverted, with 13 panels (out of a total 24) split from apex to periphery, meaning I had only half a round reserve parachute open above me. I continued my descent earthbound at a great rate of knots, the small amount of intact parachute offered me very little lift and no amount of PLF training could spare me the type of landing I was surely going to make if I hit land. Fortunately for me, due to the winds blowing from the sea towards the show ground, Steve and I had exited the aircraft far out to sea and it was a relief to know that my landing would be a watery one rather than touching down on hard ground. As my heavy, black para-boots neared the sea's surface, I pulled firmly on the red toggle on the RFD life jacket I was thankfully wearing underneath my parachute harness. The RFD life jacket, an essential and mandatory piece of equipment, was worn when parachuting close to water whether a stream, lake, water-park, reservoir or sea and although bulky and cumbersome underneath a parachute harness, on this occasion I was most happy (and lucky) to be wearing it. The life jacket inflated immediately and in the next split second I hit the water with a massive splash. I heard a loud 'fffffffssst' being the sound of my burning hot smoke canister making contact with the cold sea water and at the same time I gasped in short, shallow breaths. The life jacket inflated underneath my tight parachute harness and in doing so crushed my ribs, restricting my lung expansion and limiting my air intake to an absolute minimum. With parachute and lines entwined like spaghetti around my body, the thought occurred to me that unless a rescue boat launched quickly I might not survive. Strong under-currents pulled my parachute downwards and at times I had difficulty keeping my head above the rolling waves splashing down onto me. Steve, who had dived out the aircraft with me just minutes earlier, watched the catalogue of events from aloft while underneath his parachute and landed on the water's edge where he quickly took off his equipment, stripped off his jumpsuit and swam to my rescue.

I was a long way out, about 400 yards from the beach, and in the skies above me another ex-Team member, Sgt Sherdy Vatnsdal, had observed my parachute's fast descent into the sea so he immediately abandoned his formation flight with the rest of his Blue Eagle helicopter display team to hover directly overhead with skids practically on the water's surface where he assessed my situation. Giving the thumbs up to Sherdy to indicate I was OK, I frantically waved him away due to the downdraught of his rotor blades which created forceful spray preventing me from breathing. Sherdy flew his Scout helicopter away and re-joined the rest of his display team where they continued with their scheduled aerial display; however, I doubt there was anyone left around the arena to watch as everyone was at the water's edge waving at me as if what I'd done was part of the show. I waved to them for help, and they waved back even more.

By the time Steve reached me he was gasping for breath himself and grabbed hold of my life jacket to stay afloat. After a few minutes the freezing waters around us went lukewarm for a few comforting seconds and I owned up to Steve that I'd just done the biggest wee I'd ever done in my life and he was swimming in it. We nearly choked with laughter at the surreal situation we were in, bobbing about in my wee while waving to the crowds on the beach and to add insult to injury Steve asked, "Is this the first time you have had a malfunction?" "Yes!" "I know", I replied, "I'll get the beers in!"

The life boats we'd arranged to be in the water as part of the pre-show planning never arrived and after about twenty minutes we noticed a little boat approaching in our direction. As the boat pulled alongside us an elderly lady shouted to us, "Do you want a lift?" We accepted her kind and very much appreciated offer of help then Steve hauled himself up onto the side of her boat to clamber aboard. He found it relatively easy to emerge from the water being as he was dressed in only tracksuit bottom and t-shirt. I, on the other hand, was still fully clothed in my jumpsuit, heavy boots, helmet, and wearing a complete harness assembly with the main parachute still intact in its container on my back. The front mount reserve remained clipped onto the D Rings on my harness and the snap ejector chest-strap was impossible to undo due to the pressure from the inflated life jacket underneath it. With Steve and the elderly lady trying unsuccessfully to get me out of the water, I had no option but to bob about for quite some time longer until another crew-boat arrived alongside. It took an enormous effort to heave me and my heavy, soaked, equipment out of the water but eventually I emerged bruised and battered, my teeth chattering uncontrollably like those novelty wind-up gnashers. It was such a relief to be out of the water, my cold body juddered violently as if I was holding onto a pneumatic drill and I was as wrinkly and blue as a pickled testicle. The elderly lady wrapped a blanket around me and offered another blanket to Steve before rummaging into the depths of her handbag searching for something. She pulled out a stick of ruby red lipstick and placed it and a small compact mirror in my hand and said, "Tidy yourself up girl, you look a right mess!" In total disbelief, I said "Eh?" then politely declined, making subtle eye contact with Steve when we struggled to suppress the urge to laugh out loud, nearly falling overboard again trying to keep the giggles in. Steve and I were (and still are) eternally grateful to her for rescuing us, but the last thing I wanted at that moment was ruby red lipstick!

Navigating her way through moored boats we reached the dockside to be immediately welcomed by the police, fire service and the rest of my Team who had landed in the show ground arena and quickly driven the short distance in time to welcome us onto safe land. In true British fashion, someone pushed a large mug of tea into my cold, shaking hands and suddenly the world was put to rights and everything was better again.

The sea-soaked parachutes, harness and clothing were loaded into the team vehicle and we drove to Swansea Fire Station where the team of firemen hoisted them inside the fire-engine bay and hosed them down with their fire-fighting hosepipe blasting and rinsing away any residue of sea salt. Later, at the hotel, we secured the parachute apex to the external metal fire escape steps and hung the parachute out to dry overnight securing it safely so it didn't inflate and blow away.

The following morning, Sunday, at early o'clock, we laid out the parachutes in the large breakfast room causing much amusement and entertainment to the other clientele who sat munching on their full English breakfast while we kneeled on the floor packing the parachutes. Some of the clientele brought their Sunday newspapers to the breakfast tables and asked for my autograph as my face was on the front pages with sensationalised headlines. 'PARA GIRL HURTLES INTO THE SEA', the words 'HURTLED, PLUMMETED AND PLUNGED were everywhere! We didn't have mobile phones at that time and neither did my parents have a telephone in their home, so I hadn't been able to contact them to tell them of my ordeal. I later found out that my Dad had nearly had a heart attack when, on entering the local paper shop, he saw my face and read the bold headlines. Poor Dad! He thought I was dead! In show business there is no such thing as bad publicity and as sensational as the story was projected, it offered maximum exposure both nationally and internationally to The Red Devils Parachute Team's profile. My near-death experience made the team, The Red Devils, and myself, Jackie Smith, household names worldwide, and offers of national and local TV and radio interviews came flooding in.

Sunday dawned and the two shows of the day were scheduled to go ahead again. The wall-to-wall blue skies and light winds were favourable to jumping so we repeated the previous day's routine, driving to Swansea Airport where we kitted up into our jumpsuits and parachuting equipment in preparation for the first show. On this occasion every team member focussed carefully on their life jackets checking the inflation toggle location over and over again, preparing mentally 'just in case' a similar incident happened to any one of us. Once emplaned on the aircraft, we took flight again in the direction towards the Swansea Show. I make no exaggeration when I say that looking down from 3,000ft above the arena, we watched the enormous crowds surrounding the show ground area swarming like bees around a honey pot. I think the entire Welsh population were there waiting to watch us jump and perhaps witness the 'Para Girl' hurtle, plummet and plunge into the sea again. Fortunately for all of us, our parachutes opened normally and as I flew my parachute over the crowd's heads their shouting, screaming, clapping, whooping and cheering could be heard at 2,000ft. I faced my parachute into wind for landing and the place erupted into mayhem when my feet touched down on the target cross and fortunately I was the last team member to land as the crowds rushed forward through the barriers filling the arena with waving pens asking, "Can I have your autograph missus?"

Later that evening we met up with Sherdy Vatnsdal and the rest of his Blue Eagles Team in the bar and I rang the bell to offer a round of beers to everyone. Sherdy told me of a mishap he once had on a parachute descent into a show ground in Southampton, when friction from his harness during canopy deployment ignited a box of matches in his jumpsuit pocket. While descending into the arena he had to put the fire in his jumpsuit out which wasn't an easy task with the forward flying speed creating a wind draught to fan the flames! Sherdy succeeded in putting the flames out but not without suffering a large burn.

The following weekend, 8th April 1972, was also a very eventful show. The Team were scheduled to jump into the UK's largest sporting horse race, the Grand National Hunt at Aintree Racecourse in Liverpool. After checking into a local hotel, we were invited by the show organisers to walk part way around the race track with local and national press as a big public relations exercise promoting the team and the Grand National.

One particular cameraman (there's always one!) asked us to climb on top of Becher's Brook and jump off the top so he could capture some action shots of us leaping into the air doing star-fish positions. I doubt too many people have climbed and stood on the top of Becher's Brook but it is the most famous fence on the Aintree Racecourse standing 5'6" tall with a wide brook on the landing side. Time and time again we climbed up the jagged hedge, balanced precariously on the top then jumped spectacularly up into the air in a 'star' position so that the photographer could get his perfect shot. He asked us to do it again, and again, and again, and again, at which time we were all getting threaders and pretty naffed off with his request for more. Pathetically, he pleaded, "just one more time, perleeeeease" and a team-member's voice piped up behind me and said, "If he asks us to climb up there one more fucking time I'm going to punch his fucking lights out!" The photographer heard the comment and stepped backwards away from us, lowered his camera from his face and said in a chirpy, happy-happy voice, "Actually, chaps, I think I should have my perfect shot after all!" We could smell his fear and the lads burst out laughing at his sudden change of mind.

After the exertion of jumping and tumbling on the race-track for the good part of the morning, we decided to return to the hotel and grab a bite to eat but as we approached it in the team vehicle we were stopped by the police. At first we thought we'd been pulled over for speeding again but when we stopped a policeman approached the driver's open window and informed us our hotel had been evacuated and sealed off after receiving a bomb threat. Although our personal clothing and bags were still inside the hotel, we fortunately had taken our parachuting and DZ gear with us to the racecourse for the photo shoot, so it was with us inside the rear of the vehicle. Thanks to the public relations session earlier we were wearing our team jumpsuits, boots and beret so had everything we required for the following day's show had we not been allowed to enter the hotel. The police escorted us to another 'safe' location where we had overnight police protection; our team vehicle however, was impounded into police safe-keeping where it could not be targeted on the open roadside. Aware of the possibility of being sitting ducks should anyone attempt to shoot at us whilst under our opened parachute, the decision to jump (or not) was seriously considered but it was a general consensus that we carry on as normal and jump into the display with the positive attitude 'in for a penny, in for a pound'. Our plan of action when our parachutes opened was to perform erratic turns in each direction and not be a sitting duck under a static and smooth-flying parachute. Was I scared? Yes, I was! Yanking on alternate steering toggles I dinged and donged like a church-bell clapper, my body swinging and swaying on an unpredictable flight path to the landing area. There was an enormous police presence in and around the race track and once our Para-boots touched terra-firma in front of the Grandstands, we were whisked away in Black Maria vans. On that particular occasion we did not perform the after-jump Team line-up or shake dignitaries' hands and it was such a relief to drive out and away from the exposed racetrack. The good news that day was the horse I backed for £5, an outsider named Well-to-Do, came in to win at an enormous 33-1 and I was rich beyond belief.

During my first year on the Team, we performed over 300 parachute displays and shows around the country at various Fetes, county shows, galas, army shows, tattoos, weddings, agricultural and air shows, at all of which my parachute opened correctly without any further incidents. My 200th jump was my 54th demo jump and was very special to me as Lord Mountbatten, 1st Earl of Burma, was the special guest and he came out to meet the team at our end of demo line-up. He shook my hand and I couldn't believe someone from the Royal Family had even spoken to me, let alone for him to press palms with me.

Model shoot

Being a member of the Red Devils afforded me the privilege of meeting some incredible people with access to locations I could only dream of, and being wined and dined in the finest restaurants. As the only female, I was asked to do TV shows and interviews, local and national radio chat shows, various commercials and on numerous occasions, was invited to Helena Rubinstein's London salon where I was pampered luxuriously with amazing facials, manicures, and made up with most expensive beauty products. On a few photographic shoots I was taken to Peter Gordino's house to select a collection of clothing from his dancer's wardrobe then driven to George Harrison's house where we used his photographic studio. I couldn't believe for one minute I'd ever visit one of the Beatles' homes, but George was very down-to-earth and friendly, welcoming us into his beautiful house and happy to show me his newly designed and painted fireplace depicting an Indian mural. I was pinching myself thinking I must be dreaming, but it was all for real... I didn't overstep the mark and ask for George's autograph but wish I'd had the nerve to ask to have my photograph taken with him. Oh for a mobile phone and selfie stick in those days!

Fitting in

From my initial intake into the all-male environment, it was evident I had some serious learning to do when it came to the close-knit 'brotherhood' behaviour and lingo. There I was, a lone female, deeply embedded in hairy-arsed Paratrooper territory where their day-to-day lives continued as normal regardless of my presence. Who'd have guessed there were so many pet names for genitalia! Everything was referred to as 'Harry this' or Harry that' and initially I wondered who the hell this 'Harry' was but soon learned the lingo! There's Harry Black (polish), Harry Threaders (tired), Harry Goppers (ugly), Harry the Hat (non-airborne), Harry Sippers (posh drinkie poos), Harry Shiters (very drunk). 'Harry von' said before a word increased the poshness depending on the establishment we were drinking in. Paras don't get tired; they instead are 'chin-strapped', 'hanging-out' or 'totally bollocked'. Dirty laundry is Dhobi and Dhobi dust washing powder. 'Ally' is 'well cool' and 'Ally as F#*k' is the dog's bollocks. Non-airborne types are labelled crap hats or legs. Officers are known as 'Ruperts'. Military helicopters were given names; Aroldite Pursuit Ships and C130 Hercules affectionately labelled Fat Albert. If Sergeant Major went ape-shit, then a low profile should be kept to avoid being torn into and having one's head ripped off. We covered everything in fablon and used gorilla snot (glue) long before it became a brand name. A 'beasting' was a hard physical endurance torture test usually accompanied by a harsh verbal tongue thrashing. 'Mincing gear' is smart gear to well... generally mince about in and look posh. As a team we had uniform 'Mincing Gear' to take on the road with us. The blokes wore smart grey trousers (I wore a mini-skirt), navy blue blazer with wired and beaded Red Devil badge emblazoned on the left breast pocket, smart blue shirt, and Red Devil tie. On shows where we stayed overnight for any period of time, we changed out of tracksuit and jumpsuit into our team mincing gear and mingled as guests in a multitude of nightclubs and smart venues as VIPs all over the country, looking as smart as carrots. We used infantry methods of silent communication with just hand signals and if a team member put the fingertips of one hand on the top of his head it was a signal to 'come here'. We used a 'mark-one eyeball' to spot the aircraft and a hand slicing over the throat meant to 'cut' i.e. throttle back (aircraft engines). All instructions ended with 'Roger, Over' and usually finished with 'Out'. To 'thin out' was to disperse. Beds were 'pits' where you knocked out zeds, sleeping bags were fart sacks or green maggots and if you offered to get the 'wets' in you were buying the drinks. Hot drinks were made uniformly as NATO standard (white with two sugars) and scoff was eaten with gobbling rods and racing spoons. 'Oscar Mike' meant we were on the move, 'twos up' meant you wanted to have a turn, a go, or a read of something, their bums are affectionately called 'grinners' and when they carried out their ablutions went for a shit, shave, shower and shampoo in that order. To land heavily under a parachute was to cream in, stoof in or that familiar Harry bloke came into it again (Harry Von Stoofers). Whingers, whiners and complainers got a serious bollocking and told to stop dripping or bellyaching (expletives deleted here). When it comes to cooking you can forget celebrity bake-offs! Paras have exquisite culinary skills and can knock up a most delicious Airborne Stew, the recipe for which consists of everything in an army compo box (military field rations) thrown into a mess-tin and heated over a Hexi Stove. Treacle pudding, custard, chicken curry, oatmeal block, soup powder, brown biscuits, hamburger and beans, processed cheese, babies' heads (steak and kidney pudding), mixed together with curry powder. Field cooking at its best and absolutely delicious!

Playing pranks on fellow team mates was a time-honoured tradition and no-one was excluded, including me! On a long journey up to Scotland, we stopped at a service station for a comfort break and coffee. I made my way through the crowds and people stopped to stare at me but that wasn't out of the ordinary, particularly when dressed in Red Devil tracksuit and beret. I entered the toilet and heard other women commenting "Did you see her?" and again, didn't think anything of it, until that is, I opened the cubicle door and saw my reflection in the mirror and didn't recognise the person looking back at me. I looked like the masked killer in Scream. It was risky business taking a nap and while I'd slept in the back of the vehicle, the lads had drawn black marker pen over my face but at least they hadn't shaved off my eyebrows. I learned to always check that my boot laces weren't tied together after taking a snooze and I never, ever took my boots off and left them unattended either as they usually ended up filled with shaving foam or worse still discovered other little 'surprises' below the shaving foam. We were all permanently on hot-spoon alert in the brew room or when drinking a boiling hot cuppa for fear of someone taking a hot metal spoon out of their hot drink and placing it on your arm or neck.

On a trip to Cyprus for a winter training trip to Kingsfield airstrip, the team arrived at Heathrow for a British Airways flight. On arrival at the airport a team member's girlfriend, who worked for British Airways, arranged for the team to be upgraded to First Class. The team were escorted like royalty en masse to the first class lounge and the mother of all bars which just so happened to be free and telling the guys to have a drink but not to kick the arse out of it was a waste of breath. With three hours to wait before boarding, the word went around to screw the nut, with a general consensus reply of, 'Yeah right'! After three hours and quite a few light ales later, the lads lugged as much duty frees from the free bar as they could carry and chinked their merry way up the gangway, pouring themselves onto the aircraft. During take-off Sharky swiftly fell asleep, at which time, the Team Sergeant Major, Bob Baker, who was sitting next to him, decided to amuse himself by drawing all over Sharky's face in black ink. Later, Sharky woke up needing to take a leak and made his way to the loo. On the way down the aisle he came across a little old dear struggling to get a case down from the overhead compartment so reached up to help her. When she turned around to thank Sharky, she let out a loud, high pitched, blood curdling scream which made everyone jump out of their skins and at which time the entire flight was looking at Sharky like he had two heads. Sharky was oblivious to why everyone was looking at him until that is, he entered the toilet and saw his reflection in the mirror.

I discovered quite early on that farting is a form of male bonding while women have a more dignified relationship with trumping. As we are all aware, gas has a tendency to expand at altitude and when one of the lads passed some seriously disgusting gas, it of course sent the others into fits of laughter, each attempting to match the call. On some occasions the air was so pungent it made me gag and nearly throw up so I didn't get mad, I just got even, letting slip some sneaky rose-scented love puffs into the equation. Occasionally, Sgt Major Ted Lewington banned all farting while climbing to altitude threatening to charge anyone who disobeyed his strict order. The smells continued however but no-one dared admit ownership and all fingers pointed to me! Laugh! We nearly fell out the aircraft laughing so hard.

After heavy drinking sessions in the town we ate in some of Aldershot's finest dining establishments, namely the Cannon Indian restaurant, or Toni Louigi's Burger Bar. Once seated inside the Cannon restaurant the manager locked the doors, not to stop anyone else entering but to deter paratroopers, especially those wearing trainers, doing a runner without paying. The lure of excitement was too much for some who made a break for it escaping without paying but always did the honour of returning, sometimes a day or week later, to pay their bills. It wasn't about getting a free meal; it was all about the chase. Extreme curry eating competitions took place most nights and some threw down the gauntlet challenging everyone to eat the hottest and spiciest meal. The formidable atmosphere was one of asbestos-lipped, sweating paratroopers forcing mouthfuls of hellishly fiery curry past their burning lips into their mouths meanwhile throwing pints of beer down their necks in an attempt to cool down. It was a sight to behold, one of stinging eyes, sweating faces and mopping of brows until the last grain of rice was devoured. There is no victory without pain however and everyone complained of their burning ring of fire the following day with cries of 'Medic!' from the men's toilets.

Daytime uniform for Team members was Red Devil t-shirt, tracksuit, Para boots, Red Beret and jumpsuit. Out of work 'uniform' was the generic airborne attire of t-shirt, green bomber flying jacket, Levi jeans and sand coloured desert wellies. We lived in each other's pockets, jumped, ate and slept together (not literally) so each evening after a good day's skydiving it was the law to go out together for a few 'wets' into one of Aldershot's airborne-only pubs. Non-airborne rarely dared to venture into an airborne pub and only ever did so when the Paras were out of town on exercise, on a peace-keeping tour or at war somewhere around the world. In the pub, Team members could be observed standing on one leg, the other leg held out aloft behind them, pint of beer in one hand, arms in the 'frog' position demonstrating their freefalling position and at the same time swapping lies about when something hadn't gone to plan on the last jump. "No shit, there I was, I was just going to dock!" There was usually no video evidence so no-one could dismiss the blatant fibs, but everyone in the bar talked better skydivers than they actually were on occasions. It was all just so much fun anyway and it didn't matter if a skydive didn't go to plan, it just meant someone had to get the beers in for messing up.

One major problem I experienced on a regular basis when I joined the team was living in the WRAC female accommodation, The Duchess of Kent Barracks, where rules and regulations were very strict. All female soldiers had to sign out when going out of barracks in a book in the guard-room, then sign back in again, before the curfew of 22.00hrs. If female soldiers arrived at the guard-room any later than the curfew, then they found themselves in front of the Squadron Officer Commanding the following day. Also, if any female wanted to go away for a weekend (for me it was skydiving) it was mandatory to apply every week, by Thursday, for a weekend pass, signed by the Officer Commanding. Imagine the problems I encountered returning from a long day on the road, after jumping into up to five show grounds across the country and returning to camp later than the curfew after a long road journey. It was never the same guard commander and I had to explain and beg to each and every one of them on every occasion I returned late to camp that I was with the Red Devils. I found myself on report on more occasions than I can shake a donkey's tail to. I also missed weekly room inspections and found myself on orders for not being there to open my bunk door to the inspection team. I applied to live out of the barracks but it was declined as it wasn't something afforded to junior rank females but I was unofficially allowed to find alternative accommodation off camp but claiming living out allowance was another hurdle to jump over.

Tightening my leg-straps

It took a further two years of Major Schofield's endless negotiating with the establishment for me to receive living out allowance during which time I paid for my food and accommodation in the Duchess of Kent Barracks but never slept or ate there. At least it gave me the freedom to come and go at whatever unsociable hours being on the team demanded, without interrogation from a guard commander every time I returned to camp. I showed my face in the Duchess of Kent barracks at every opportune moment to catch up on Part 1 and Part 2 orders, give my room a spring clean, and check in with the OC 3 Sqn who accepted and appreciated I was in a very unique place in the military, a lone female under the Parachute Regiment's umbrella.

En-route to a show ground

alongside me with blue light flashing. The police officer opened the car door, stood to his feet and shouted, "Excuse me Ma'am! Why are you walking on the verge?" I was totally nonplussed and looked around to see if there was anyone behind me that the police officer was talking to. The police officer became more insistent and asked again, "Ma'am, why are you walking on the grassy verge?" I assumed that where I was walking was out of bounds and asked, "Where else should I be walking if there isn't a pavement?" He stopped dead in his tracks, scratched his head, and looked at me like I had two heads, not understanding a word I'd said. "Huh?" "Excuse me, ma'am? Are you from London, England?" I answered, "Yes, I'm from England and am walking to the Golden Knights' accommodation!" His eyes popped wide and he took off his police hat, "Oh, Ma'am! Are you really from England? I love your accent! Say something! Gee, Ma'am, I've never met anyone from England! You have such a cute accent. Say something!" A pattern was beginning to emerge and again, what do you say when someone asks you to say something? He told me I sounded like a movie star and completely captivated by my 'neat' and 'cute' English accent, he offered to drive me in his police car to the Golden Knights facility. I told him I was in the military and parachute training with the Golden Knights but I'm sure he didn't listen to my words, only to my lilting accent. So excited to meet someone from England, he kept asking if I'd met a prince or princess and did I know The Beatles. I didn't want to disappoint him and burst his bubble by admitting I wasn't really a movie star, wasn't famous and was raised on a council estate nicknamed Slaggy Island in the north of England.

His patrol car came to a halt outside the Golden Knights' team room where everyone was in preparation for morning PT. The police officer escorted me out of the vehicle and Major Schofield thought I was in trouble. With the US Team leader, Chris Needles, he asked, "What's the problem, officer?" Both Team Commanders sighed with relief when the police officer said he picked me up because I was walking and it was something local people didn't usually do. From that day on I waited at the BOQ for the duty driver to drive me as I didn't want to cause any more commotion.

The Golden Knights and the Red Devils Team mustered in loose formation outside the accommodation block dressed in our newly issued grey sweat-pants and sweat-shirts bearing 'USA Army' emblazoned on the front. Our first physical training session commenced with what was to be our daily dose of US Military exercise and we jogged in formation to the First Sergeant's rhythmic holler, "In cadence... Exercise!" We Brits had no idea what 'in cadence' meant so we went with the flow copying the Golden Knights' every move chanting along with the loudest of them and enjoying the camaraderie. "HUT, TWO, THREE, FOUR...HUT, TWO, THREE, FOUR", then all around our American hosts chanted returning cadence;

(I made this up!)

"Jackie Smith is a friend of mine,
We do PT all the time,
Push-up, sit-up, two mile run,
We don't stop until Jackie's done."

Each day we drove out to Pope Air Force Base (AFB) and had a variety of jump aircraft lined up for us to use. We jumped mostly from Hercules C130s as there were so many of them to accommodate large numbers on each lift, with us Brits, the regular USAPT members and their team try-outs who were hoping to be selected as full time members of the Golden Knights. Other aircraft options were CH47, Otter, DC3 or Huey helicopters, and daily we flew out to the Golden Knights' training drop zone at Camp McCall or Laurinburg NC where we parachuted throughout the day. The DZ was an enormous sandy and grassy airfield with triangular tarmac runways, the whole airfield was surrounded by dense and tall pine trees which filled the air with an unforgettable fragrance. The DZ was bare, with nothing other than the catering wagon with our lunch and drinks, a few portable loos and a massive hole which we help dig out to dispose our used smoke canisters after jumping. The packing area was a large concrete square with hooks as tensioners for packing round parachutes and this was also where we busied ourselves during the day sitting, laying, eating, and drinking between aircraft lifts. Throughout each day the Hercules picked us up, climbed to altitude, threw us out at the top (16,000ft) and repeated for as long as there was daylight.

The Hercules C130 is affectionately known as Fat Albert and in my opinion is the most exciting aircraft to jump from whether launching from the side door or the wide, gaping tailgate to run, dive, and somersault from. Each time we jumped the C130 we came up with novel exits to see who could do the best forward or backward somersault. Some pirouetted off the edge or stood 'to attention' saluting rigidly as they fell away into the slipstream but the best fun exits I ever performed was a balancing handstand placing my fingers over the tailgate outer edge like a diver on the high diving board, kicked my legs into the air and balanced for as long as possible before falling over the edge into the forceful slipstream. The C130's running-in speed on jump-run was faster than freefall terminal velocity (120 miles per hour) and my first (yes, I got the beers

Fort Bragg – waiting for the C130, my taxi to altitude

in!) tailgate exit was more exciting than any skydive I'd performed up until that point. The slipstream didn't hit me initially; it was a second or two after launching from the tailgate that the blast of air slammed into me taking the air out of my mouth before pinging me across the sky like a rag doll. What fun!

Contradicting those who ask why I jump out of perfectly serviceable aircraft, here is a description of a not quite so serviceable aircraft. The speediest exit I ever made was over St Mère Église DZ in Fort Bragg where before take-off, the Huey helicopter pilot briefed the six fully kitted-up skydivers what action to take should the helicopter encounter engine or other flying problems. The pilot emphasized the urgency of exiting the helicopter as quickly as possible if there was a problem but highlighted we skydivers should not freefall for longer than ten seconds

With Golden Knights and Tryouts 1972

before deploying our parachutes. His 'no-more-than-ten-second-rule' meant that the parachutes opened high, giving him clear airspace to auto rotate below and to avoid his flying into us. He indicated that during autorotation he had limited control over the helicopter's flight path as it rotated down towards the ground. In a helicopter, an auto-rotative descent is a power-off manoeuvre in which the engine is disengaged from the main rotor system and the rotor blades are driven solely by the upward flow of air through the rotor. We climbed aboard the Huey and I sat in the open door with my feet dangling over the skids watching the sand and earth swirling wildly as we lifted off the ground. The altimeter needle indicated we were at 9,000ft when the helicopter started throwing us around violently and the pilot shouted, "Emergency! Exit, Exit, Exit!" We skydivers didn't hesitate diving out the door putting his earlier and well-timed emergency briefing into swift action. Sitting underneath an opened parachute at a higher than normal altitude we scanned the dense woodlands below trying to locate a safe area to land. The DZ was too far away in the distance to attempt landing on and putting our accuracy skills to the test was interesting landing together in a miniscule clearing between the tall pines. The helicopter pilot, a Vietnam veteran, landed the helicopter successfully creating a huge cloud of sand on the edge of St Mère Église DZ and fortunately he was unhurt.

The Golden Knights took The Red Devils under their wing, sharing not only their skydiving skills but also demonstrated their expertise in drinking games. If parachuting wasn't going to kill me when I was with the team, then surely all the drinking games should have. One particular drinking game separated the boys from the men (me included) and involved a ritual of drinking a pitcher of beer while performing precise word sequences and table tapping. I claim no responsibility for anyone trying this game and prepare for a mega hangover attempting.

Kitted up, ready to go

The Real Cardinal Puff Rules! Drinking Game Rules

Start with a full pint (or pitcher) of beer. The objective: finish the glass in six tries, and leave no drips – the penalty for such will be revealed later, so read on. Grab the pint glass with your thumb and forefinger and hoist to face level. "I drink to the honourable Cardinal Puff for the first time." Consume as you can (remember there are five more drinks from the same pint, so don't drink too much). Tap the glass, once on the bar top then set it down. With the fore finger of each hand, tap the bar top (alternating left/right), tap the underside of the bar top, tap each thigh top, tap each thigh back side, tap each foot, stand up, then sit down once. Grab the pint again, hoist aloft using thumb, index and forefinger and toast "To the Cardinal Puff Puff, for the second time." Take two drinks, tap the glass twice on the bar top, and use two fingers and repeat the first step (tap, tap, etc...). On the third go, the player (or victim) will say, "I drink to the Cardinal Puff, Puff, Puff, for the third and final time." Hoist the glass using thumb and three fingers and consume all remaining beer in three separate drinks (making sure there is virtually none left in the glass). With three fingers, repeat tapping sequence (three times each). Upon finishing tapping sequence and sitting sequence, the subject needs to grab the glass with an inverted grip and proclaim "Once a Cardinal, always a Cardinal, never spill a drop!" While proclaiming this, the player inverts the glass, releases the grip and inverts (to upright) again. There should be no liquid from the glass on the bar from the inverted pint and if there is... FAIL! Repeat the whole process again! If there is no liquid, the ruling Judge asks the subject; "Are you a Cardinal?" To which the subject shall reply, "You bet your sweet ass I am!" Any other answer is unacceptable and constitutes FAILURE and repeating the whole process again. If, in future times, you are approached and asked "Are you a Cardinal?" The only answer can be, "You bet your sweet ass I am." The person asking the question may then challenge the other person by saying, "Prove it." The person MUST prove they are by doing the whole process before you. They in turn, can ask the same of you. To make the game more challenging from the basic level of Cardinal Puff, the following are rules for advancing in the ranks. Cardinal – One pint glass. Bishop – Two pint glasses, the first glass fully consumed on round one, then parts two and three on glass two. Arch Bishop – Three pint glasses, one for each part of the game. To make Pope it is a pitcher of beer. So, if you asked if I am a Cardinal I'd reply, "Bet your sweet ass I am" but I doubt very much I could prove it or even attempt it again now.

Our British accents alone took on celebrity status and we were invited to all the airborne forces bars at Fort Bragg, the main and favourite being the 82nd Airborne Club whose team leader and 1st Sergeant was Spider Wren. Spider was a master hand at painting canopies and used a sponge and dye technique to paint designs on surplus all-white parachutes, his own being a huge black spider. His parachute club also had a pea-gravel pit (landing area) bearing the same spider design in it which was surrounded by tall pine trees and located at the rear of the 82nd Airborne Club bar. Spider invited the Red Devils to an 82nd Airborne Club BBQ and party but threw down the gauntlet challenging us to jump in and land in the small spider pit to gain entry to the BBQ. In true competitive spirit we accepted the challenge, fully aware of the miniscule landing area and lack of alternative landing areas, apart that is, from in the tall pines. An audience of 82nd Airborne club members and invited 18th and visiting 101st Airborne Division skydivers gathered to witness 'the Brits do or die' by jumping into the BBQ and as daylight faded into dusk, we exited the Hueys at 5,000ft in one long drawn-out pass. One by one we approached Spider's pit making our entrance, some landing with more finesse than others who arrived unceremoniously into five yard PLFs skidding and burning across the ground to rapturous applause, whooping and laughter. Our prize for landing in Spider's Pit was his famous Spider Pit Badge, an award not many skydivers achieved, and I have to admit that my experience of the challenge is right up there rating in my top ten buzz factors.

Fort Bragg was a huge cultural experience for us on that first trip and although our language was similar, some of our English words meant something totally different over there. During an accuracy competition at Raeford, we sat around the pit watching the competition and one female landed fast and hard scattering the pea-gravel everywhere. After the dust settled she stood up, patted herself down and shouted loudly, "God-dam! Mah fanny's sore!" Shocked, we Brits looked at each other in disbelief at what she said. It was a 'nudge, nudge, wink, wink' moment then someone from the Red Devils shouted, "Blimey, she must have had a good time last night!" The rest of us just fell around in fits of laughter but the Americans were totally nonplussed as to why we laughing.

Thanksgiving approached and each Red Devil was invited to a Golden Knight's home to celebrate on that day and over the long weekend, and Sgt Joe Pelter asked me to join him and his family for dinner, warning me not to eat anything before arriving. We sat down to dinner and apart from the turkey which was the size of an ostrich on steroids, I didn't recognise any of the foods on the table and had never seen or heard of them before. There was scalloped oysters; browned butternut squash; cranberry sauce; tangy tomato aspic; hashed brussels sprouts with poppy seeds; creamed spinach; home-made corn bread; honey butter; pumpkin pie; pecan pie and platters of assorted cut-up fresh vegetables, cheeses, meats and dips spreading across the huge dining table. The portions of food on my plate alone was more than my whole family back home would have eaten in total over a weekend. Not wanting to be rude, I tucked into everything sampling the new flavours and before long I was so bloated I thought I was going to explode. Joe and his wife were the perfect hosts, plying me with innocent-looking beverages, tall glasses of delicious eggnog. My legs disappeared from underneath me when I stood up and it was then I discovered the drinks were loaded with alcohol, a whole bottle of bourbon. We retired to the lounge where Joe and his family watched the big game of American Football on a cinema-size TV (everything in America was huge it seemed) but the game made no sense at all to me and as much as I enjoyed the atmosphere I fell asleep, inebriated, and didn't wake up for hours. Joe gave me his recipe for the Eggnog and if you wish to indulge I take no responsibility for the outcome as it is delicious and very more-ish. The recipe is here: 6 eggs, 2 extra egg yolks, 4 cups of whole milk, ¾ cups heavy cream, ½ tablespoon of sugar, ¼ teaspoon of salt, 1 tablespoon of vanilla extract, ½ teaspoon grated nutmeg and the 'pièce de résistance' being a bottle of bourbon (a large bottle, that is!)

Prior to our return to the UK, the Red Devils were invited to perform a parachute display from a C130 with the Golden Knights at Fort Bragg's Main Post Parade Field which was an amazing experience. Landing in the arena we formed a joint team line up of Golden Knights, Red Devils and the try-outs who had been selected to join the Knights. With great pride I stood to attention, saluted a Three-Star general, shook his hand and on behalf of the team presented him with a Red Devil baton, a token of our appreciation for the hospitality extended to us during our stay at Fort Bragg. The military and civilian press agencies were all over me like a cheap suit because at that time, I was the only female on a military team in the world. Later that evening at the Golden Knights ceremony, Captain Chris Needels presented to me a framed certificate congratulating me on becoming an honorary Golden Knight, an honour of which I am so very proud. I must have made an impression on the US military big wigs because three years later the US Department of Defense took on the task of selecting a female to join the USAPT Golden Knights, cue Cheryl Stearns who, in 1977, became the first female member of the US Army's elite parachute team.

On our return to the UK it was suggested by the military powers that I undertake military parachute descents at RAF Abingdon as a Public Relations exercise, the intention was for me to jump clean fatigue. I commenced synthetic ground training with other nearly airborne infantrymen who were in the final stages of Parachute Company (P Company) training qualifying for their Parachute Regiment Airborne Wings.

After four days of ground training, harness training in swings and trapeze to simulate in-flight drills and PLFs, I was summoned to the Wing Commander's office and given the news that the RAF hierarchy had decided that I should cease parachute training and not be allowed to complete any military descents from military aircraft due to there not being a female toilet on the C130 jump aircraft. I was really disappointed and although I'd completed many C130 jumps in the USA, I was denied the opportunity because of a 'no female convenience' clause which I think they made up to keep the door closed to other females. Major Schofield however succeeded in obtaining authorisation for me to attend a day of lectures, medical examinations and decompression tests in the Oxygen Chamber with the lads on the team. The decompression run simulated being at 25,000ft where we sat in a chamber wearing oxygen masks and aircrew inner helmets. Individually we were instructed to turn off our oxygen supply when our physical changes became obvious due to becoming hypoxic through lack of oxygen. I wasn't aware of what happened at the time but found it increasingly difficult carrying out the simplest of tasks of solving very basic additions and take-aways using pen and paper, when the writing I was able to put down on paper became very large. The medical officers conducting the training monitored very closely everyone's condition and when the oxygen was turned on again, I gradually resumed the simple tasks and after about ten seconds my writing returned to normal size. After the training finished, the doctor discussed the symptoms we'd all experienced emphasising the importance of recognising our own personal symptoms of hypoxia and the importance of others around us, to also recognise another person's hypoxic state.

Many years later, the RAF relaxed their rules, and I was allowed to complete a few military static-line jumps from C130 onto land, and a couple into water at Poole Harbour. This amazing event was arranged by Major Gerry O'Hara for the entire JSPC staff and their wives (if they were interested). It had taken a long time from when I was declined the parachute jump in the first place when I was a member of the Red Devils. I will be forever miffed by the RAF's decisions not to let me jump from a C130 due to there not being a female toilet. I could

Closely judged by Dicky and Scotty

never make the grade required to become a member of the Parachute Regiment for the simple fact that I did not have the physical strength and endurance required. Passing P (Parachute) Company training is arguably the toughest basic training in the British Army and I certainly wouldn't have wanted any concessions made because I was female.

On more occasions than I could count, I witnessed the blood, sweat and tears dripping from Parachute Company lads returning to barracks after their incredibly physically challenging tactical exercises and team events on Wellington, Hungry Hill, 7-Sisters and Flagstaff Hill on the Aldershot training ground and tank tracks around Long Valley. It certainly sorted out the wheat from the chaff and in order to earn the maroon machine (Red Beret) they had to dig deep to sustain tough mental and physical endurance, while being told their pain was just weakness leaving the body. There was not a chance in hell I could have passed that test, kept ahead of the knot in the log race, or in fact any of the other physical (and mental) tests required to pass P Company training unless it was watered down to accommodate my female form and weakness. The only way I could pass the Stretcher Race would have been if I was laid on the stretcher and carried around the five-mile course. Parachute Regiment soldiers parachute into their target objective carrying rocket firepower and heavy mortars strapped to their bodies (the mortar base-plate alone weighed approximately 130lbs), then on landing, TAB (tactical advance to battle) long distances to enemy attack points whether on exercise or for real in theatre. The numbers of men who meet the Parachute Regiment's physical and mental standards are miniscule and the chances of any female passing P Company's physical and mental challenges would, in my opinion, be a rarity unless the bar is lowered and concessions made.

Marooned

After two and a half years on the team, the military hierarchy deemed I should be honoured to wear the Parachute Regiment's Red Beret as my posting to the team was a permanent attachment for an indefinite amount of time. Of all the parachute demonstrations I ever did, the ceremonial Red Beret presentation jump was one with the highest profile and media interest which, on the day, turned out to be one of the most embarrassing moments of my life. The landing area for the parachute display was the grassy strip between the main road (Alison's Road) and the Dakota aircraft which stood proudly in front of Depot the Parachute Regiment Browning Barracks in Aldershot. It was a huge PR day not only for the Red Devils but also the Parachute Regiment, the Women's Royal Army Corps and the British Army in general. The world's press, national and local TV and Radio awaited my arrival by parachute, to capture the moment in history, the presentation of my Red Beret by General Sir Richard Nelson 'Windy' Gale GCB, KBE, DSO, MC who served during both World War 1 and 2. It was such an honour to receive the Red Beret from such an eminent member of the Parachute Regiment. The parachute descent was organised and the plan was for a fellow team member, Sgt Deak Wright, to pass the maroon beret to me in freefall with Steve Slater as aerial photographer, then for all three of us to land in front of the Dakota. There, I was to hand the maroon beret to General Gale for him in turn to present to me and place on my head.

At 6,000ft the aircraft flew on jump run into wind and on the wind-line from the military stadium, directly overhead the Dakota outside Browning Barracks and towards Normandy Barracks Gymnasium. The winds were marginal (blowing a hooley) but there was no way we could let the weather beat us on such an enormous occasion. We took a long, deep spot (exit point) and Deak and I dived out the aircraft and immediately went unstable, our bodies making glancing acquaintance with each other like a pair of underpants in a tumble dryer. We stabled out, made contact in freefall when Deak passed the beret to me but not before giving me a kiss pass and then tracking away from each other to open our parachutes. I was low when I pulled my ripcord, then my parachute decided to yawn and snivel for a second or so before opening. The ground looked particularly close and I immediately steered my parachute in the direction of the Dakota landing area but knew right away I didn't have enough altitude to cover the distance. I tried everything possible to increase my canopy's forward speed, undid my chest strap to allow my parachute to expand slightly, lifted my

Escaping the compound... with a helping hand

legs high up on my chest to reduce drag and ridiculously sucked air into my mouth attempting to draw myself closer to the landing area. I knew sucking the air had no effect anyway but hanging helplessly under a parachute I was game to try anything. My parachute ran out of altitude and didn't cover the distance across Alison's Road, so I had no option other than to land in the 1 Para Logistics and 63 Para Sqn REME workshops compound, an area totally fenced off with very high wire. To avoid landing on the numerous military vehicles parked inside the compound, I flew my parachute cross-wind (not advisable) then stoofed in spectacularly on the concrete floor grazing my knees, elbows and hands as my forward momentum pushed me faster than I could run.

The stinging sensation in my gravel-filled grazes was really painful but pain was not on the agenda, there was a highly decorated General and the world's press awaiting my arrival on the other side of the fence just twenty feet away. I unclipped the side alligator clips, unhooked the reserve parachute from the harness chest D-rings and let the pack fall the ground. Stepping out of the harness I retrieved my beret from inside my jumpsuit and raced towards the compound gates which faced away from the awaiting press onto Montgomery Lines Parade Square. My day went from bad to worse when I discovered that the compound gates were locked and all the military bods had gone to the cookhouse for scoff. I shook the heavy metal gates in total frustration, the rattle so loud it brought two of my military skydiving friends out from a portakabin office located inside the compound and I can't express how happy I was to see their two faces! Fortunately for me, Lt Tom Macartney and Sgt Martin Togher (Togsy) had remained in the compound through their lunch-break and observed my unceremonious landing. Brave Martin climbed over the 15ft fence first as 'catcher' on the other side, meanwhile, I clambered onto Tom's clenched hands when he hoisted me up to scale the fence. The crotch of my jumpsuit snagged on the top of the fence and as I jumped down into Togsy's arms my jumpsuit gave way and I ripped a small hole, fortunately not big enough to expose my backside. My face was as red as my jumpsuit as I came to a halt directly in front of General Gale where I slammed my feet together, stood to attention before saluting smartly. In a hectoring loud voice General Sir Michael Gale said, "Glad you could make it girl!" I replied, "Thank you Sir! Women drivers for you, Sir!" General Gale threw back his head breaking the deafening silence with a loud, cackling laugh, patted me firmly on my back and placed my Red Beret squarely on my head. It was an immense moment in time, becoming the first female in British history to wear The Parachute Regiment's coveted Red Beret, an honour of which I am exceedingly proud. My military headdress from then on was the Red Beret with Women's Royal Army Corps cap badge. In today's modern army many females wear the Red Beret if attached to Airborne units but never with the silver 'wings' cap badge which are only worn by elite members of the Parachute Regiment. I was allowed however, to wear those silver wings (and gold lanyard, presented to me on a Parachute Regiment parade, for achieving 1000 jumps) on my Number 2s uniform jacket.

A very special Red Beret day

Life on the Team

Giv'us yer autograph missus

Letting the public get involved

In 1972, after my first 'hairy' show with the Team, Jackie Smith became a household name and each show I jumped into from then on, presented crowds wanting to see the 'girl' who had hurtled, plummeted and plunged to near death into the sea in Swansea. Not only that! I was the envy of every red-blooded female on the planet spending my every day in the company of fabulously fit and handsome uniformed soldiers. Women wanted to be with them; men wanted to be them. Children swarmed around like bees to a honey pot shouting "Missus, missus, give us yer autograph" so I developed a very quick 'Jackie Smith, Red Devil' scribe to enable me to get on quickly packing my parachute on the edge of the show ground arena. There were so many people asking for autographs, photographs, press asking me to pose with parachute I embraced every opportunity to exploit the Red Devils' profile (in the best possible way of course) grasping every press, TV and radio reporter to maximise the military as a recruiting opportunity. Asking the audience for a volunteer created stampedes of kids where I was in danger of being crushed in the rush. Jostled in amongst the pushing and pulling there were cries of, "me missus, me missus" "pick me missus, pick me". I'd choose the nearest kid and seat him/her on the parachute container on the ground and use them as an anchor weight when I could keep the parachute lines taut while I flaked, folded and pleated the parachute canopy. During the packing sequence, I talked to the crowd explaining what I was doing and the reason I was doing it and they really appreciated the interaction. Excited kids were keen as mustard to be involved and many asked how they could do a parachute jump and join the army to be just like me. The icing on the helper's cake was letting him or her insert the final ripcord pin to secure the parachute pack closed and I imagine those kids (and grown-ups) bragged for a very long time about the day they helped the Red Devil girl pack her parachute. Whoever the helper was, always got a special reward from me, a Red Devil pack containing signed photographs and posters and my reward was seeing big, smiley and happy faces. On each and every occasion I packed my parachute at the side of the arena, when the parachute was folded, the pack closed, ripcord pins in place, straps and buckles tucked safely away, someone in the crowd who had just watched the whole packing sequence would, without fail, ask me, "Who packs your parachute?" I did a lot of tongue biting but always responded professionally, smiled sweetly and answered the question as if it was the first time I'd ever heard it. If I had a pound for every time I was asked that question I'd be a multi-millionaire.

It was essential we pack really quickly after each show because more often than not we had further parachute displays to do the same day, sometimes up to seven, and usually at all four points of the compass across the United Kingdom. An example of a busy show day on the Team: Manchester Army Show (2 x displays each day) into the same arena, one early then the second much later in the day. In between the Manchester Army Shows was one show at Congleton Carnival, two at Southport Flower Show and the last show of the day being the Great Yorkshire Show at Harrogate, Yorkshire. We jumped into the Manchester Army show at 11am, landed in the arena, did the team line-up and shook hands with the dignitaries, quickly repacked the parachutes and mingled briefly signing autographs. The team driver was always chasing our backs shouting, "Come on, hurry up" as he had to get us from A to B to keep to our tight schedules. We climbed aboard the team vehicle which the drop zone (DZ) party had driven to the arena from our base in Aldershot. After each show the DZ party struck (cleared) the arena/drop zone clearing and packing away all used and unused pyrotechnics, communications equipment and any other team debris into the Team vehicle, ferried the parachutists to the next emplaning airfield where the aircraft had landed. The DZ party then drove at break-neck speed across the country to arrive at the next show ground to set up the next arena with target cross and new smoke flares for the next show. The ground crew's presence in the next show ground was essential and until they arrived and displayed the target cross, the parachutists in the aircraft couldn't jump. Without the ground crew there would be no-one to manage the arena, light the ground smoke flares or to give a commentary, so occasionally we parachutists had to circle overhead hoping not to overrun our air clearance window until the show ground was ready to receive us. The hectic schedule was the team's routine for every show on every show day, usually every weekend and bank holiday from March until late October and we were so tight for time between shows, we didn't eat or drink until after touching down on the last show of the day. After the team line-up on the last jump we raced, like big kids, pushing and jostling in the direction of the nearest hot-dog/burger/pie vendor where we literally rammed anything down our necks and refreshed our raging thirsts with a pint (or three) of beer. Those last-jump-of-the-day beers were essence, nectar of the gods (sky-gods in our case) which didn't touch the side, gone in one almighty gulp. After a day of rushing from arenas to airfields, jumping and packing, we were sweaty and usually wearing smoke-tinted orange faces and hands. The pungent orange smoke seeped through our protective jumpsuits and outer clothing and every team member sported matching orange underwear, socks and t-shirts, the colour stain never, ever washed out, not even on the hottest, whitest wash. We all had matching orange nasal hair and eyebrows too which was many a topic of conversation on team line-up as it looked like badly applied make-up or fake tan. Some show organisers invited the Team into the VIP tents where we mingled with celebrities, taking the opportunity to indulge in whatever food was available, but usually it was small portions, posh canapés and tiny nibbles which was never enough to satisfy the blokes' bottomless pits and enormous appetites. We were all Hank Marvin, the blokes moaned constantly that they were so hungry their bellies thought their throats had been cut and finding a burger stall or fish and chips shop was first and foremost on our minds before setting off on the long road journey back to Aldershot. The rear of the team vehicle, which had mounds of unpacked parachutes, served as somewhere to lay and get our heads down to sleep while some played cards, Crazy Eights or Canasta as the team driver used huge maps to navigate home to Aldershot.

One particularly lengthy journey for my Black Team was to jump into the Motorcycle TT (Time Trials) Races on the Isle of Man which we did every year; meanwhile, the Red Team, with the assistance of guest jumpers from the other airborne units, had five other shows around the UK on the same day. The Black Team consisting of seven parachutists, two DZ party and driver, departed Montgomery Lines in Aldershot at very early o'clock and travelled in the team's diesel Commer Van which had a governor attached, restricting it to a maximum speed of 47 miles an hour. Journeys were painstakingly slow and on the lengthier journeys up and down the country, we tied a long piece of string to the governor and whoever sat in the passenger's seat pulled on it for the entire journey to increase the vehicle's speed to an amazing break-neck speed of 53 miles per hour.

Those extra six miles an hour faster were a godsend. The Commer Van was a bread van which Postman Pat would have been proud to drive and not only was it slow and cumbersome, but incredibly noisy too. The diesel engine clattered and knocked so loudly we couldn't hear ourselves speak on journeys and the only time we broke into conversation, was when the vehicle was coasting downhill and it became blissfully silent. On one occasion, Scouse (Albert Owens) put the gears into neutral and we careered headlong down a long decline, the vehicle picked up speed, enough to enter the outside lane to overtake for the first time in the vehicle's history. It was such an amazing event to be overtaking other vehicles in the Commer Van we cheered loudly, yahooing and jubilantly punching our fists in the air. Our excitement was short-lived however when a police car with flashing blue lights and siren blaring cruised alongside indicating we pull over. Scouse applied pressure to the brakes and steered onto the hard shoulder; meanwhile we were booing and hissing in the back of the van. It was the stuff that pantomimes are made of, we were heckling the big, bad policeman but on that occasion he turned out to be not so bad after all. The police vehicle pulled up in front of us and the copper approached the driver's open window popping his head inside to take a look at us as we sat like obedient school children in total silence. With his head inside the window the police officer said, "Do you know you were doing 59 miles an hour in a 50 mile an hour limit?" to which we all erupted into over-the-top, manic cheering and yahooing celebrating a new speed record for the Commer van. Scouse even had the nerve to thank the police officer for giving us that information as we had no idea the van could travel that fast. The police officer gave us a warning, allowing us to continue our journey but before he left, we gave him a Red Devil pack with brochures and signed photographs for his little boy. It was a win-win situation.

The logistical planning for the TT Races in the Isle of Man was complex. The Black Team's emplaning point for the show was at Manchester Ringway where we hired a Britten Norman Islander from Northern Executive Aviation for the drop. The Red Devil's own aircraft, G-AXDH was being used by the Red Team to carry out the other five demos elsewhere around the country. At the team room, the Black team prepared the equipment for the day ahead, berets brushed, boots polished, jumpsuits washed and ironed, team t-shirt and track-bottoms, parachutes packed ready to go, helmets cleaned of orange smoke stains and boot scuffs, smoke bombs loaded and tightened into jubilee clips on the brackets. As ambassadors for the Army and Parachute Regiment, we were always turned out as smart as carrots and were subject to pre-demo inspections to ensure we came up to inspection uniform standard. We set off at 3.30am and after the long journey north the driver and DZ party dropped off the skydivers at Manchester Ringway then continued the journey by ferry to the Isle of Man. Before kitting up we checked with the ATC the weather conditions and it didn't look favourable that we would jump as storms were forecast. We learned from experience that weather forecasts were not always accurate and if we didn't fly and try, we might have had the embarrassment of not jumping in glorious weather conditions. The pilot flew the aircraft the eighty or so miles across the Irish Sea and after a short time, we disappeared into the darkness of black clouds. It was hard to tell which way was up and which way was down with no horizon and rain lashed horizontally past and into the open door soaking those sitting closest to it. Pockets of turbulent air unseated us parachutists from the hard aircraft floor throwing us violently up and down and from side to side. If any one of us had been accidentally ejected out of the aircraft or had the misfortune of doing an emergency exit, the lashing waves below would have swallowed us up. It really was the worst flying experience any of us had endured and I know I wasn't alone admitting I was scared. The full English breakfast I'd eaten earlier that day came close to making a reappearance but fortunately didn't. Eventually, and to our relief, we saw the Isle of Man coastline and shortly afterwards we were over land again when the TT show ground came immediately into view. Cloud base was about 400ft above the ground and the pilot flew the aircraft slow and low over the arena, while Ian Christie dangled his leg out the door while firmly holding onto the strong-point inside. The ignited orange smoke strapped to Ian's ankle blazed an orange trail behind the aircraft, meanwhile, the rest of us huddled in the open door frame, again holding firmly onto the strong-point, and waved to the rain drenched and disappointed TT Race crowd below. With the parachute descent cancelled, the pilot headed the aircraft back across the Irish Sea again towards Manchester Ringway and again we experienced the same turbulent conditions. The DZ party in the TT Races arena packed up the DZ equipment, loaded it into the Commer Van and returned by ferry to the mainland and Manchester Ringway where we waited, for hours and hours, to be picked up before setting off for the long, slow journey back to Aldershot. It really was the longest day on the road and no parachute display to show for it.

After the events of such a long day, you'd be forgiven for thinking nothing else could possibly go wrong, but in typical Murphy's Law, it did. On the journey south, the Commer Van ran out of fuel and Scouse eased the vehicle over onto the hard shoulder. Tired and dejected and still dressed in our Red Devil jumpsuits we sat on the top of the motorway bank while Scouse disappeared into the night carrying a Jerry can in search of a garage which were few and far between. After what seemed like an eternity, Scouse returned with the diesel and poured it into the vehicle using a Mark 1 funnel made out of the TT Race demo's op-order. When Diesel engines run out of fuel, air gets trapped in the system and when the engine is started, the air acts as a lock, preventing the normal supply of fuel. 'Someone' had to bleed the air out by sucking through a long, straw-like tube until only diesel remained in the tank and all air removed. If air remains and is trapped, then the engine simply will not start. It really wasn't Scouse Owens' day and because it was his bad admin and judgement not keeping an eye on the fuel gauge, he was volunteered as that 'someone' who had to 'suck it up, sunshine!'

He knelt down and began sucking the air from the fuel pipe while we urged him on with childish banter and sexual innuendos like "Oh Scouse, where did you learn to suck like that?" With one almighty suck, Scouse got a mouthful of diesel and swallowed the lot in a big gulp, his eyes nearly popped out of his follicly-challenged head. While he proceeded to spit out and regurgitate the contents of his stomach onto the side of the road, the rest of us fell about laughing uncontrollably rolling about on the grassy verge. He wiped his mouth, but his ribs continued to involuntarily retch and he made the stupid mistake of asking, "Come on lads, where the fuck do I find some sympathy?" In the darkness, a very northern and sarcastic voice piped up, "In the dictionary between Shit and Syphilis!"

Emplaning at Manchester Airport

Show Time

Life on the team was a routine of endless opportunities, travel and adventure where every weekend was either show-time at parachute displays in arenas all over the UK and abroad or competing at national and regional drop zone competitions. Thursday evenings in the Team packing room the Red, Black, Competition Teams and guest jumpers attended a briefing session to discuss the upcoming weekend's activities. Details of each show were chalked up on large blackboards with both ground crew and air party schedules for each show, identifying locations, estimated times of departure (ETD), parachute hours (P hour), aircraft positioning point, NOTAM and height clearance, jump manifests listing individuals jumping on each show and order of jump exit, arena information highlighting potential hazards and who we would be meeting on the team line-up. We also checked if there was any elevation above or below sea level differences from departure airfield to arena landing point to make necessary adjustments to altimeters before take-off. Without the constant support of the guest jumpers from the other airborne units, the Red Devils' heavy weekend display schedules would not have been possible and taking on less shows would have meant less publicity for the team and also less income into the Team's coffers.

In the early 70s, before parachuting commenced, the aircraft door was removed leaving a gaping hole into which the cold, icy wind whistled around us as we sat, sometimes for hours, flying to various show grounds. On one occasion we emplaned and took off from Farnborough airfield where at ground level the temperature was -5 degrees and the ground was covered in a blanket of snow. Fully kitted up we climbed aboard and huddled tightly, sitting on the hard floor behind the pilot for a lengthy flight in a piston aircraft to a show ground in Scotland. The two people sitting directly behind the pilot's seat were toasty warm due to the heater being underneath their backsides whereas others seated at the rear of the aircraft, next to the open door did everything possible to stay warm by donning balaclavas, neck warmers and motorcycle gloves. During the warmer, summer months on long flights to show grounds when the aircraft's noisy engines drowned out any form of normal conversation other than shouting, I sat in the open doorway looking out at the changing scenery below where windswept cornfields resembled choppy seas and the clouds' shadows moved swiftly over the landscape below. Some team members read the daily trash newspapers ogling page 3 girls but one very smart Alec, Nish Bruce, flicked through the Daily Telegraph newspaper before tackling the crossword which he completed easily and within a very short time.

Nish had a very funny experience at the hotel in Newcastle where each year we jumped for a full week, twice a day and this is his story. At all the shows we jumped into, the lads were a big hit with local girls especially when they were wearing their team jumpsuits around the show ground and it wasn't unknown for certain team members to milk their pulling power by remaining in their jumpsuits after each show until we returned to the hotel each evening. Dressed in a Red Devil jumpsuit more or less guaranteed even the least handsome team members an exchange of contact details whereas back in Aldershot, wearing their 'out-of-uniform' uniform of jeans, desert-wellies, maroon top and sage green 'bomber' flying jacket had little to no chance of scoring with any female. On the road, the girls hovered like flies around the proverbial hoping to make acquaintance with the team members, meanwhile men looked on in envy.

When the daily show was over, we were usually invited for drinks at night clubs being celebrated like royalty and never having to pay for drinks or food. It was a tough life but someone had to live it. One team member let it be known to some girls where the team were staying and later that evening, the hotel bar was in full swing with many local females ready to pull and party. Everyone was having a good time getting drunk and Nish thought it a good idea to impress the girls by wearing the gorilla suit which was inside the team vehicle along with the rest of the equipment. He staggered out of the bar and hotel main doors and unpacked the gorilla suit which he had been wearing earlier when he jumped into the show at the Town Moor. Dressed in the gorilla suit, which looked incredibly real, especially with the full-faced and hairy helmet head, rubber gorilla hands and feet, he returned to the hotel where he found the doors had locked behind him when he left the building. In the days before mobile phones, Nish had no way to contact the barman or anyone on the team who were all too busy having a good time chatting up the girls to even notice he was missing. Nish sat down in the flower bed opposite the hotel to consider how he could gain entry and in the cosiness of the hairy gorilla suit fell into a deep alcohol-induced sleep and snored the night away.

The next morning Nish woke up in the flower bed, opened his eyes and found loads of police staring down at him along with a vet and primate expert who had been summoned from the local zoo. Earlier at 5am, two nuns on their way to prayers at the convent had stumbled across Nish and fled in terror alerting the police to a huge gorilla sleeping in the flower beds. The whole area was sealed off and apparently the police discussed firing a gorilla-strength tranquilliser into Nish's furry arse. Nish sat up with a start and started talking to the police and rifle-toting vet explaining he was a Red Devil parachutist at the same time as removing the gorilla head and mask. When Nish's identity was established as a human, not a gorilla, a police sergeant asked, "Who's your commanding officer?" Lying through his teeth and trying to avoid the police contacting the Team Commander, Captain Micky Munn, he replied "Captain John Street!" John Street was another team member with the rank of Private and Nish's ploy was to avoid Micky Munn finding out what he had done. Not much chance of that! The police summoned the hotel manager from his bed and unfortunately for Nish he woke up Mickey Munn. Micky arrived at the flower bed where Nish was still sitting and still wearing the gorilla suit. He was absolutely furious and tore into Nish reading him the riot act which fortunately was drowned out by the police sirens. The whole area was like a crime scene with blue flashing lights whizzing up and down the street as police cars and fire engines pulled up alongside to contain the on-the-loose gorilla. Nish narrowly avoided being shot with the gorilla-strength tranquiliser but had the wrath of Micky's punishment to deal with but not before jumping again, as the gorilla, into the show ground later that afternoon.

The buzz of jumping into big show ground arenas is immense where the crowd's cheering is amplified in a fish bowl arena. Each team member, on landing in the arena, took off their parachuting equipment and laid it on the ground taking care when releasing the smoke bracket and hot smoke canister and placing it on the ground a safe distance from the parachuting equipment to avoid any burns. The team line up was as important a display as the actual parachute jump and added the smart military element the public enjoyed. As a finale we formed in line, usually facing the dignitaries' area, standing 'at ease' in front of the Team Leader who bellowed out "Teeeeeeam... Team-shun!" Heart pounding from the excitement of the jump, we slammed our feet together as we did on all military parades, to attention. We were proud to be there at each and every show we performed, regardless of its size or audience, be it a small village fete at one end of the spectrum, or perhaps the Grand National with millions of spectators watching on TV. Not only were we smart as carrots but we were usually coloured like carrots too, a result of orange smoke streaming from the smoke canisters on our ankles up our bodies and into our faces when the parachutes opened. The dignitaries at each show were introduced to individuals in the team line-up and offered handshakes, some enthusiastic double handed, others firm knuckle-crushers and some limp and lifeless like a damp lettuce leaf. After the exchange of pleasantries, the Team Leader, for maximum effect for the crowds' enjoyment, shouted at the top of his voice again, "Teeeeam! Fall out!" In military fashion, we turned sharply to the right, saluted smartly in unison, leaned forward (as if into a stiff breeze) anticipating the first step forward before breaking into a run, each member peeling off towards their own personal equipment lying somewhere in the arena.

The Team Headquarters in Montgomery Lines (barracks) Aldershot was part of a large building which also accommodated the airborne intelligence cell and military education centre. Our accommodation consisted of two offices and a rigging room, where various activities took place like equipment manufacture, canopies modified or repaired, hot knifing materials, general stitching, leg swinging (hanging about) and most importantly, making brews. The entire Montgomery Lines accommodation was built for males with not a female loo in sight (apart from in the nearby Naafi) so when I paid a visit to the ablutions I'd stick a 'Ladies' sticker on the outside door for privacy. More often than not however, the lads ignored the notice on the door and I was often confronted with someone hanging out in the urinals. The parachute packing room had two long narrow tables on which main and reserve parachutes were laid out, flaked, folded and packed. There was a lot of blood, sweat and tears on those tables

Instructing Junior Parachute Regiment soldiers

with a lot of teddy bears thrown into the corner from the frustration and exertion it took to close the tight and unforgiving parachute packs we used at the time, particularly the Super-Pro container. The tables were flanked on both sides of the room by tall grey lockers where each team member kept his individual parachuting and personal equipment and essential cans of 'instant bath' (deodorant) which we sprayed energetically to disguise the hum of armpits wafting around the team room after long days on the drop zone.

Opposite the Team admin office was the Parachute Equipment Stores where Sgt Joe Grieg ruled supreme, issuing equipment to all and sundry on military 1033 forms. In the main entrance masses of trophies and memorabilia were displayed proudly in showcases and glass cabinets, exhibiting for all to see the Team's achievements at numerous military and civilian competitions throughout the Team's existence. Our preferred place of work, the drop zone on Aldershot's Queens Avenue, was located a short distance away and weather permitting, we jumped our bums off daily using the team's Britten Norman Piston Islander, G-AXDH as our taxi to altitude. We jumped from light o'clock 'til dark o'clock, pausing only briefly when the aircraft flew into Farnborough airfield to refuel. The team's aircraft was flown during our parachute training days and also on

Training Junior Paras

shows by keen 'volunteer' airline pilots, Roger Mills, Ed Murray, Roger Brown, and many more who enjoyed getting their hands on the controls of smaller, lighter aircraft after flying in their full-time day jobs in Boeing 747s or supersonic Concorde aircraft.

My 'day' job when not parachuting was everything administrative where, in the hub of all activity, the Team Sergeant Major Ted Lewington, Colour Sergeant Laurie Casey and the Team Clerk, Sergeant Dave Sands, Sgt Jim Petherbridge and myself kept the office engine cogs in motion. It was a hive of activity, an extremely busy environment with a variety of visitors coming and going, TV, radio and press, and military and civilian skydivers dropping by to use the team's facilities, borrow equipment or simply have a brew.

The team room had ONE telephone in the office which at the time must have been the hottest telephone line in British military history. It never ever stopped ringing and in the days before answer-phones or mobile telephones, the team had no technology for anyone to leave a message, so goodness knows how many missed opportunities there were due to no-one being in the office to answer. Besides my daily call from Sergeant Major Nobby Arnold, most callers were show organisers across the country requesting a parachute demonstration at their county show, agricultural show, flower show, carnival, fete, donkey derby, water jump or wedding! You name it, we jumped into it and our motto used to be 'You call, we fall!'

Approximately 20 annual KAPE (Keep the Army in the Public Eye) shows were mandatory commitments scheduled into our annual total of demos when we jumped into Army displays and passing-out parades up and down the country. Some of those shows included the Royal Navy's Field Gun Runs at Portsmouth and Royal and International Military Air Shows such as Biggin Hill, Farnborough and Duxford. Billed as the 'highlight', we usually parachuted into each show ground as the last event of the day and from the show organisers' point of view, he retained the masses, 'Joe Public', inside the show ground thus maximising his financial opportunities until the end of the day.

From the moment we took a firm booking for a parachute demonstration, the planning and organisation wheels went into motion. A Team member took on the responsibility of recce-ing the proposed show arena to inspect its locality noting any major and minor power lines in the vicinity or, water, rail line, anti-parachutist trees, anti-parachutist fences or poles, and note any potential hazard to parachutists. The proposed parachute arena also had to conform to the

British Parachute Association's minimum arena size with show organiser's guaranteed crowd control in the form of fences (to keep the crowds out of the parachutists' landing area) to avoid collision and injury to anyone. The recce team sketched to scale a drawing of the arena and its surroundings and all information relating to each display was filed manually in the enormous grey metal filing cabinet in the Team Office. How much easier it would have been to file electronically using today's modern technology with computers, internet and social networking. Landowner's permission had to be obtained in writing to allow parachutists to land on his property (to avoid being prosecuted for trespassing) and local police were notified of our estimated time of arrival (ETA) or Parachute 'P' hour.

When one team, say, the Red Team used the team's own aircraft and the Black Team had displays on the same day, we hired other chartered aircraft but those aircraft and its pilots had to have clearance to drop parachutists. There is a fine art to piloting a parachuting aircraft, not only safely at the correct flying speed and correct level, but also flying the aircraft accurately over the drop zone on the wind line. On jump-run the aircraft should always be flown flat and level, not nose up or nose down, and at a steady 70 knots. If the aircraft flies too fast or is slightly nose up, there is a risk the parachutist could hit the tail-plane and cause not only serious damage to himself but also to the aircraft. We never disputed any pilot's flying skills, but on the odd occasion it took a lot of patience on the jump-master's behalf to direct the pilot to the correct flight line allowing us to exit in the correct place. Fortunately, those forward-facing pilots were never privy to the cursing going on behind them or hear the frustrated swearing which was drowned out by the engines. Not only was the sky blue on those occasions but also the air inside the aircraft! For each parachute demonstration, the Civil Aviation Authority (CAA) were notified of the 'P' hour and number of manifested parachutists to jump. The CAA allocated a timed 'window' of parachuting opportunity and maximum flying altitude issuing a NOTAM giving us total air clearance flying to and from the airfield and in the general airspace over the show ground area. The last thing a parachutist wants to see when he is just about to jump from the aircraft door is another aircraft flying underneath; the NOTAM gave the team a time framed window allowing the parachutists and aircraft to be in particular airspace and 'should' restrict any other flying activity during the time given. Occasionally however, we encountered a 'bandit', a rogue aircraft, encroached in our airspace when we were about to jump and fortunately were spotted by either our keen-eyed pilot or jump master before we exited the aircraft avoiding possible collision in freefall.

Parachute displays didn't always go to plan and individuals occasionally had the odd 'cock-up' and landed outside the show ground due usually to unforeseen circumstances when the main parachute malfunctioned. Every year we jumped into a show ground in Goole, Yorkshire. Ted Lewington had a very lucky escape when his parachute, a long-lined Para-Plane (square canopy) malfunctioned, carried out his emergency procedure, cutting it away (to jettison it) before deploying his round reserve parachute. Round parachutes, especially reserve parachutes, were classed as life savers and not necessarily limb-savers as precision landings were not usually an option. Unfortunately for Ted, his round reserve parachute drifted towards some high tension National Grid power lines which he failed to avoid landing on. On the plus side, Ted's feet didn't make contact with the ground but if they had, he would have earthed himself and been fried, electrocuted. For a long, long time Ted dangled helplessly from the high tension wires, meanwhile the fire brigade, police and others watched from underneath unable to rescue him until the National Grid turned off the power. The Boothferry Bridge (a swing bridge), was fully open allowing shipping to pass through on its way to Selby when the National Grid switched off the power to allow the rescue services reach Ted. After the rest of us had landed in the show ground completing the team line-up without our Sergeant Major, we made our way to where Ted was suspended and joined the rescue teams. While Ted was dangling helplessly he took a fair amount of flak from the rest of us, "What's the view like up there Ted?" and "Come on Ted, stop all this hanging about?"

It took a few hours for the rescue services to lower him to safety and to also retrieve his reserve parachute which was snagged over the power lines. Once safely on the ground and detached from the power lines the National Grid switched on the power again allowing the swing bridge to close with much relief to the gridlocked town of Goole and surrounding road networks. The team received a hefty bill in the region of £10,000 for the inconvenience but Ted himself paid the heaviest penalty in embarrassment and also physically. Throughout the ordeal Ted had been suspended under the power lines, his entire body weight slumped down into his parachute harness leg straps resulting in crushed and numbed nuts. For a good week or so, Ted walked like a cowboy and stood himself down from jumping as he couldn't bear any pressure on his groin from the parachute harness.

Brazil

Shortly after being presented with my Red Beret, the Team were invited to represent Great Britain at the International Air Show at San Jose Dos Campos, Brazil. At the end of a hectic weekend of shows involving the usual dashing to and from arenas and airfields in our red 'E-type Commer bread van', we arrived exhausted at Aldershot at around 02.30 hrs on Monday 10th September. There was no time to go home to sleep as there was only 12 hours before we were due to jet off to the land of sun, sand and señoritas in Brazil. Needless to say though, no-one complained about missing out on blanket pressing and we worked through the night unpacking the team vehicle of weekend show debris and refilling it with essential kit for the trip. Pyrotechnics (smoke canisters) initially presented a problem to our luggage, being listed as 'hazardous air freight' but Sgt Major Ted Lewington's various contacts and abilities of organising the impossible had them transported by our 'blue job' friends, the RAF Harrier squadron from Wittering. The next problem was to transport ten Red Devils, including one dolly bird (me), one gorilla (Jim Petherbridge) and all our kit to Sao Paulo for the duration of the International Air Show held at San Jose dos Campos. Air France trolley dollies wafting heavy Parisian perfumery into the reconditioned air served us wine and croissants and Bob Harman charmingly entertained them all with his schoolboy French and charming, flirtatious hand kissing. In true chat-up style, he took hold of the air-hostesses hands (as he did with every female he met), tenderly kissed it then impressed them with his well-rehearsed chat-up line, "Bonjour mademoiselle. Je suis Bob Harman des Red Devils. J'ai plus de 1000 sauts!" Bob was such a smoothie and a genuinely polite and personable bloke. I've seen him at parties, stand to attention in front of a VIP, salute, then do a side left (or right) PLF and it never failed to impress as a party piece.

Within an hour of touchdown in Paris and many more renderings of Bob's schoolboy French, we managed to board the correct aircraft at the correct time – destination Brazil. On Varig Airlines' inaugural flight we flew from London to Rio de Janeiro, and for the fifteen-hour flight were treated like royalty, complimented with Varig's incredible in-air hospitality. Next stop was Rio de Janeiro, or at least that's where we thought we were heading. Instead, we diverted and landed at Recife due to the aircraft nearly running out of fuel. After a few hours hanging around the airport we were airborne again, the aircraft flew south on its 2,500-mile journey and eventually we landed on Rio de Janeiro's airport runway which stuck out like a huge pier over the sea. Those of us not sleeping looked out of the small windows in total disbelief at the beautiful scenery below us. It looked like Paradise! On touch down we gathered our baggage and stepped off the air-conditioned aircraft wearing our team mincing gear, the lads in blazers, grey trousers, shirts and ties, myself with skirt and over-the-knee black suede boots. Phew! It was like stepping into a furnace once outside the aircraft with soaring temperatures like we'd never experienced before and, dressed for our British winter, we were all dripping with sweat and finding it difficult to breathe as we made our way down the aircraft steps to the terminal. After a short while we were climbing another set of steps boarding our connecting flight to Sao Paulo. As we were taxiing out towards the runway again, Deak Wright looked out the window and noticed our distinguished-looking red and black baggage and parachuting equipment being thrown onto a trailer which was then driven off towards another aircraft bound for another destination. We thundered at great speed down the runway for take-off and shrugged our shoulders relishing the thought of a three-week holiday in Rio without any parachuting. Major Peter Schofield, the Team Commander, had scheduled his flight to Brazil a few days earlier than the rest of us and had carried out the necessary recces and arranged PR coverage with press, radio and TV. As a result, the entire Brazilian nation were aware of our impending arrival but what they didn't know was we had no parachutes to jump into the air shows. We thought we might face the firing squad for not fulfilling our commitments at the air show but that idea was put temporarily out of mind by an absolute barrage of press and TV who filmed, photographed and interviewed us for hours to the great inquisitive pleasure of a busy airport terminal building crammed with locals waiting to see us. I imagine it as similar to a pop stars' reception but the locals weren't thousands of gorgeous young females ripping their clothes off shouting "I love you" to the blokes, they were chanting my name, "Jackie Smith, Jackie Smith, Jackie Smith, Jackie Smith". The rest of the team watched from a distance as the press and TV mobbed me and I overheard Bob Harman comment to the media (who didn't understand a word he said), "It's OK! The rest of the team are just here to make up the numbers!" The reason I was the focus of attention was I was the first female skydiver and also first female soldier ever to set foot in Brazil. My arrival was big news in a country where females were second class citizens and traditionally chained to the kitchen sinks, babies and housework where their Latino husbands assumed masculine superiority.

The coach ride from the airport to the hotel was unbelievable on the heavily congested and badly maintained roads. How we didn't crash is a miracle. There appeared to be one rule for all road users and that was to speed along as fast as their vehicles would go whilst honking their horns totally disregarding everyone else on the road. Crossing the road became a major challenge when we were out and about on walkabouts. We plucked up the courage to cross the street in front of the hotel and stood in a line as if at a race starting point. The front, 15-deep line of cars stopped at the pedestrian crossing and as we were two thirds across and beyond the point of no return the green light illuminated indicating the cars to go. Like a Grand Prix starting grid the vehicles surged forward towards us and we had to sprint like Olympiads at break-neck speeds to avoid being run over. Bob Harman, in his mad dash using what little adrenalin he had left in him after the sprint, just made it to the other side of the road after doing a one-handed leapfrog over the bonnet of a 'not-about-to-stop' VW Beetle. Safely on the far side of the street we congratulated each other's survival and decided to celebrate (any excuse) and drank Brazilian cocktails until the early hours of the morning when the traffic eased enough for us to risk crossing over to our hotel side of the road again.

In the heart of Sao Paulo, the third largest city in the world with a population pushing 20 million, we were accommodated in the multi-storey Tropical Hotel Planalto along with most of the other military show participants from the USA and UK including the RAF crews of the Nimrod, Vulcan and Harrier, the crew of the American C5A and also the USA Army Parachute Team, The Golden Knights. The accommodation, with its air conditioning, booze filled refrigerators; telephone and TV was a far cry from some of the cheap B&Bs we frequented when travelling up and down UK on local shows.

The following day Ted Lewington once again used his authoritative muscle and organised the recovery of our lost baggage and parachuting equipment and accepted the keen hotel porters' offer to carry everything to our rooms. The porters, who we tipped generously for their services, found out the hard way how heavy our parachuting bags were and they were very wary to offer to carry anything else for us during our stay from then on, avoiding us when we arrived and departed each day.

For a couple of days, we acclimatised and lived the high life, sampling expensive foods and bottomless glasses of champagne, wines and local brews, sight-seeing, visiting gift shops and generally getting used to the eye-watering atmospheric pollution. Most Sao Paulo neighbourhoods were easily explored on foot but we adopted the 'safety in numbers' rule when going out to bars and restaurants as each street corner had youths hanging around and a multitude of very young prostitutes selling their wares.

At early o'clock on the Friday, all team members dressed in red trimmed and badged black Team tracksuits, white running shoes and maroon berets, made our way to the coach which was awaiting us outside the hotel. The crowds gathered as we were leaving and having answered umpteen times, "No" to the question, "Are you a football team?" we were on the bus once again for a one-and-a-half-hour journey to San Jose Dos Campos. The airfield was way out in the country and free from the congestion and pollution of Sao Paulo and we were greeted by a few uniformed gentlemen armed with six-guns in their leather gun-belts similar to the vintage western style sheriffs I'd seen in cowboy movies. Some of the police guards carried rifles too.

The heads of the parachute teams participating in the air shows, the Red Devils, The Golden Knights and Brazilians; Major Peter Schofield, Captain Chris Needles and Major Carlos Prado respectively, went off to the show briefing to get timings for the display. They returned within the hour and because I was the only female to have ever skydived in Brazil, the decision was that the Red Devils be given the first slot of the sixteen shows to get maximum press coverage. We accepted enthusiastically and the line-up for the show in order of jump was, me out first on my Papillon, Steve Slater Para Commander, Deak Wright on the cutaway rig, Alex Scott on another cutaway rig, Jim Petherbridge on his Para Commander and jumping the gorilla suit, Dave 'Paddy' Ritchie on the Delta II Para Wing, Joe Grieg also on the Delta II Para Wing, Bob Harman and Ted Lewington on their Para Clouds and Major Schofield on his Sled. The jump aircraft was a Buffalo C115 which was a new experience for us and yes, a case of beer all around on that occasion. The first show went well apart from both the cutaway canopies disappearing into the crowd and not being returned. The pilot was excellent and needed no flight corrections on jump run and the exit point was directly over the cross with little to no wind. Flying in at 10,000ft (12,000ft above sea level) I exited, followed by Steve, then gorilla Jim and Joe exited together and spun the 2-man, candy-poling the smoke for maximum impact for the awaiting crowds directly below us. Deak and Alex tracked away from us, each gliding a safe distance apart before performing their intentional 'malfunction' cutaways and streaming the 'dummy' parachutes before jettisoning them to open their 'real' parachutes. Again, Deak and Alex trailed their smoke for maximum effect while the commentator expressed the risks both parachutists faced performing such a stunt. Major Schofield, Ted and Bob tracked in opposite directions from each other from 10,000ft creating vast distance between each other before deploying their high performance parachutes which could glide them back to the landing zone regardless of the distance they had travelled. The 250,000 audience enjoyed it immensely mainly because they had never seen freefall parachutists before. The Golden Knights were their usual professional selves making a four-man formation with a bomb-burst and diamond track which was the highlight of the show. The Brazilians, although a relatively young parachute team, performed quite a spectacular stunt which left the rest of us parachutists open-jawed when we looked skywards at their show. Three jumpers, all huddled together in the aircraft, leapt out of the door and all three ended up suspended under one parachute which was opened by static-line at around 8,000ft. From the ground it looked like one man underneath a parachute until one of the three fell away followed two seconds later by the second man. The one left behind on the parachute then streamed the parachute to make it look like a malfunction and all three fell together in freefall. The crowds screamed fearing all three parachutists were going to continue falling and hit the ground. A collective gasp of 'ahhh' rang out from the crowd when the three skydivers deployed their parachutes at a frighteningly low altitude.

A variety of different aircraft flew in the air show performing spectacular stunts and unfortunately a tragedy occurred on the practice day when a glider pilot, Scotty McRae, had to fly a borrowed glider due to his own not clearing customs in time. Scotty's show was magnificent and his final upside-down fly-by was right in front of the crowd line. Sadly, Scotty lost control of the glider as he flipped to upright position and crashed in full view of everyone.

One of the aircraft taking part at the air show was a Hawker Siddeley 748 and fortunately it was scheduled as the Red Devils jump-ship for the air shows. The HS 748, a civilian version of the RAF's Andover, holds around forty parachutists where eight can stand side by side in the wide, gaping single left hand rear cargo door. On the final day we had a unique experience when a dozen or more camera crew from Brazilian press and TV flew with us to do some in-air filming and interviews. One brave cameraman wearing a safety harness, which was in turn hooked onto a strongpoint in the aircraft, dangled outside the door frame with a white-knuckle death grip whilst fighting in the slipstream and holding onto a huge cine camera to get some decent exit footage. Behind him was his mate holding a huge frame on which two illumination devices, the size of Scammell headlights, floodlighting the inside of the aircraft. We couldn't understand why he had the extra lighting because outside the wide aircraft door was blazing sunshine. During the air show and whilst circling the airfield at 10,000ft, a Hawker Siddeley 125 executive jet flew within a 10 foot distance from our starboard wing tip and then 10 feet from his wing tip, a Harrier flew in tight formation. The three aircraft flew around in close, line-abreast formation for

In the door of the Andover aircraft in Brazil

ten minutes and from our point of view it was quite spectacular watching as wing tips nearly touched. The 125 peeled off leaving the Harrier which was literally flying wing-tip to wing-tip with our aircraft as we climbed to jump altitude. In the seat behind the Harrier pilot another cine cameraman took footage of us as we leapt out into the slipstream. When I jumped out of the HS 748 door I felt the heat from the Harrier's engines blasting me in the slipstream where I looked up and waved to the smiling pilot. Falling earthwards it was the most amazing vision, the Harrier pilot and cine-cameraman waving back at me, the Harrier itself distorted behind refracted air travelling in bending shimmery waves. Incidentally, the Harrier pilot was John Farley PBE AFC CEng who I was later introduced to, 39 years later, at a Royal Aeronautical lecture evening at Salisbury Arts Centre.

Travelling on the bus each day from the hotel in São Paulo to San Jose dos Campos was like being in the middle of a musical carnival extravaganza. The Brazilian team members were full on rhythm, singing, dancing, tapping fingers, tapping feet, clanging empty tin cans, tinkling bottles, hands drumming on any surface, the roof of the bus, seat backs, making soulful music while dancing the Bossa-Nova in the narrow aisles. Bob Harman, attempting to infuse some British music into the mêlée, sang his favourite Eric Clapton song 'House of the Rising Sun' but the Brazilians drowned out his lone voice with their carnival musical din.

More shows were organised by the British Embassy for us in Rio de Janeiro onto Copacabana Beach and into the Maracana Stadium, once the world's greatest playground for famous soccer stars. After the short flight from São Paulo to Rio we were again greeted by media and press then ferried in luxury cars to the British Embassy. The consulate staff working at the British Embassy hosted individuals in their own homes for the week and I was fortunate to be hosted with a lady whose house was a short walk from Copacabana Beach.

Sitting on Copacabana Beach's golden sands, I watched scantily clad athletic males and females exposing sun-kissed skin and all around explosions of music, dancing, volley ball and football. Christ the Redeemer towered high on the granite peak of Corcovado Mountain standing majestically over the whole city, while in another direction bubble-shaped cable cars ascended and descended the Sugar Loaf Mountain.

Unfortunately, the display into the Maracana Stadium was cancelled due to inclement weather so the rest of the team were given a day off to go sight-seeing while Major Schofield, Jim Petherbridge with gorilla suit and myself attended a press call with TV, radio and newspaper interviews. That afternoon it was announced by the media to the population of Rio de Janeiro, that the famous Red Devil's parachute display onto Copacabana Beach, would take place the following day. The Team's picture was emblazoned on billboards everywhere and the show was advertised on TV and in magazines prior to us arriving in the country and before the show Major Schofield was assured that for our safety, we would be assisted by Brazilian Paratroopers and Police when we landed. The display was scheduled for mid-afternoon giving us ample time, or so we thought, to repack our parachutes and travel to the airport to catch our homeward bound flight later that evening.

We emplaned in the Buffalo C115 aircraft at Rio's airport and flew the short distance overhead towards the beach. The aircraft was laden once more with camera crews and much to the lads' delight, a beautiful, big breasted and bra-less female reporter accompanied us on the flight. It was hilarious watching the lads forming a shambolic line before the gorgeous reporter where they waited in turn to ogle while giving her their life stories. Meanwhile, the aircraft climbed high over the Rio de Janeiro coastline flying close to Corcovado Rock and over the golden beaches towards Sugar Loaf Mountain. The cooler air at higher altitude had a very pleasing effect (for the lads) on the female reporter's nipples which stood erect like Scammell starter buttons. It did occur to me that the lads were so distracted by the reporter's attributes they might elect to stay in the aircraft and not follow me out to do the show. At 10,000ft I looked out the door at the squared-off arena, the rest of the beach appeared black with so many people on it and while I was enjoying the aerial visuals of Rio de Janeiro, the lads were focussed solely on the female's breasts (while I rolled my eyes!) Prior to the show onto Copacabana Beach Paddy Ritchie had injured his knee jumping the gorilla suit at San Jose Dos Campos so he was volunteered as the Drop Zone controller and commentator. The wind drift indicator had been thrown at 2,000ft above the arena and it was evident from where it landed that the winds were blowing a hooley in a direction from the sea towards the beach. There was no margin for error assessing the winds to land on the narrow strip of beach as the undershoot area (if we dropped short) was the rough sea with large, lashing waves; the overshoot area (if we went over the top of the arena) was a concrete jungle of high rise buildings, skyscrapers and densely populated favelas. This was one show we did not want to cancel from the air so Joe Grieg and I exited the aircraft first followed by Steve Slater and Jim Petherbridge who was wearing the heavy, black gorilla suit. Conscious of my previous 'hairy' experience when I landed in Mumbles Harbour, I was relieved when my red, white and blue Papillon opened like a dream above my head. No dramas this time! Sitting in my parachute harness under a full canopy I located the landing area checking my wind drift, ensuring I was on the wind line before pulling the orange cord to ignite the smoke canister attached to my foot. The orange smoke then gushed and trailed behind me through the skies over Rio's breathtakingly beautiful land and seascapes. From underneath my parachute I glanced upwards towards the aircraft and watched Deak perform a cutaway descent with a canopy loaned from the Brazilian Team. The two Red Devils' cutaway canopies that had gone missing on the previous shows at San Jose Dos Campus air show, were probably being used as curtains in a hacienda somewhere in Sao Paulo. Although there was a PA system on for Paddy Ritchie to give a commentary, it was about as much use as a chocolate fire-guard because the excited throng wouldn't have, even if they spoke English, been able to understand his strong Northern Irish accent. From under the canopy I watched the arena disappear when the crowds ran into it and within seconds the drop zone was totally awash with crazy people, a sea of faces looking up at me with their arms stretched upwards, shouting and screaming as I descended closer and closer towards them. Paddy was brandishing a ground smoke flare in one hand trying to establish a small area for me to land but was

I'm in there somewhere (Copacabana Beach)

overcome by the sheer force of excited Brazilians. The crowds didn't hear me shouting to move out the way, nor would they have understood me, so I had no other choice but to land on them. It occurred to me that the burning hot smoke canister on my ankle, which was still spewing and spitting out orange smoke, would possibly burn someone if I landed on their faces or heads. My feet didn't touch the ground however, my thick-soled Para boots thudded in on someone's shoulders and the chaotic mob cleared slightly as I bounced off people's backs. If I'd fallen to the ground, I'm pretty sure I'd have been trampled on. It really was the most terrifying ordeal I have ever experienced as the hysteric Latinos pushed and grabbed at me pulling on my helmet straps, parachute and ripcords hoping to steal a souvenir. I was then picked up by a group of sweaty men and they tried to drag me away, perhaps also as a souvenir. A policeman roughly grabbed me and pulled me towards a large group of other policemen. He fought with gun in one hand while dragging me through the hysterical crowd across a six lane, gridlocked carriageway to a sea-front hotel. Steve Slater was still descending towards the arena, which was no longer an arena, looking for somewhere to land and he too disappeared into the crowd. Again, the gun-toting policemen went to his rescue and dragged him out to safety. Inside the hotel

On target (and smiling)

and at the request of a local VIP, we were taken upstairs to a balcony overlooking Copacabana Beach where it really was like a scene from Evita, the crowd were chanting "Red Devils! Red Devils! Red Devils!"

Unbeknown to me at the time, Ted, who observed my descent from the aircraft door, watched the arena disappear into a mass of people and told Major Schofield the aircraft should return to the air base and the rest of the team abort the jump. Major Schofield said, "Sod that! I'm not giving up this opportunity of jumping onto Copacabana Beach for anything" and through an interpreter told the pilot to continue on jump-run. They went ahead and jumped but there was nothing but a sea of people to land on which made life very interesting for Sgt Jim Petherbridge. Jim was wearing the heavy gorilla suit which had a full-faced hairy helmet and in his thick-soled Para boots made him stand about 7ft tall and very life-like indeed. Excuse the pun but the crowd really went 'ape' when they caught sight of the gorilla descending towards them and he too had to fight his way, with the aid of the police, to escape being beaten to death. Safe in the confines of the hotel, an exhausted Jim, still fully dressed in the gorilla suit and full face mask and helmet, staggered up the stairs to join the rest of us on the balcony. In the heat of the Brazilian sunshine Jim was sweating buckets but before undressing decided to extend his fifteen minutes of fame and climbed on top of a concrete pillar on the balcony where he stood high above the crowd, threw back his head to roar, and pounded his chest like King Kong. The crowds went absolutely insane and gunfire broke out. How Jim escaped getting shot is a miracle! We didn't realise until we returned to England that the name Guerilla was a nickname for the Brazilian political assassination squad so Jim flaunting himself in front of the crowds was like waving a red flag to a bull.

A few limousines, with black tinted windows to obscure passengers' identity, arrived at the rear of the hotel awaiting our escape to take us and our equipment to the airport for our UK departure but the police deemed it far too risky for us to leave the hotel. The hysterical crowds were so completely out of control the riot police were called to disperse them and for three hours we waited until it was safe enough to make our escape. It was a frightening journey as the limos raced us to the airport and, reflecting on our ordeal, we were relieved and thankful to escape with our lives. At the airport we had time to breathe and regroup our equipment, discovering that some items were missing, three ripcords and four smoke brackets but the saddest loss however, was Steve Slater's maroon machine, his hard-earned Parachute Regiment Red Beret. Later, while we relaxed in the airport lounge, the police informed us that there had been a four-hour traffic jam in the six-lane highway and the rioting crowds we'd left behind at the Copacabana Hotel had broken three large plate glass windows and several cars had been tipped upside down in the mayhem. That was one heck of a crazy day!

At 11.30pm that evening we were airborne once again, on our way home via Lisbon and Paris and looking forward to home soil. We also looked forward to returning to our typically British events like Vicars' Tea Parties and Agricultural Shows where we could sip tea and eat sticky buns with our native audiences again not fearing the experiences of the past few days in Brazil.

More excitement was to come however. In the aircraft's relaxed ambience where we virtually drank dry the airline's in-flight hospitality, Deak Wright noticed we were circling London and assumed we were being held off by Air Traffic Control awaiting our turn to land. Three hours later our Air France 727 aircraft continued circling and our plane-load of anxious passengers sensed something was seriously wrong. The atmosphere was beginning to get very tense as passengers, told to remain seated with seat belts on, agitatedly discussed what could possibly be the problem. The pilot then announced we should remain seated and prepare for an emergency landing and before we knew it the wheels touched down. The sound of screeching brakes filled the air and everyone lunged forward in their seats before the aircraft came to an abrupt halt in the centre of the runway. The exit doors were opened immediately and the pilot announced in French, "Urgence, urgence. Laissez tous les articles à bord et abandonnez le navire immédiatement par la sortie arrière." Bob Harman shouted, "Emergency! Go! Go! Go! Leave your gear and get your arses out of here!" We made a swift evacuation down the rear hatch steps to be welcomed by a host of emergency vehicles, fire engines, police cars, ambulances and a bomb disposal unit. Later, inside the terminal, we discovered Air France had received a telephone threat from the IRA informing there was a bomb on board our 727 aircraft. For the next eight hours, security used manual search and sniffer dogs to check the aircraft with a fine-tooth comb, while we sat awaiting clearance to collect our parachuting equipment and personal items. We at last were on home soil but didn't quite expect the arrival to be so spectacular!

1973

Throughout 1973 we carried out hundreds of parachute demonstrations into just about every venue in the UK and also competed successfully at all regional, National and Army meets. One of the most exciting demo plans was to jump onto the tennis deck of the QE2. We were invited to lunch with the captain who explained how he would drop all aerials and put out sea boats as a safety measure. Unfortunately, on the day of the demo the cloud base sat menacingly at 100ft so the show was cancelled. That would have been an amazing jump for our log books!

Carrying my equipment to the packing area

Major Schofield went to Tangiers, Morocco to do a recce for a demo for the Young President's Organisation and on his first night there had to audition 50 belly dancers. This was hot news making headlines in British tabloids who slated the Parachute Regiment and 'Famous Army Parachute Team' as the UK had no diplomatic relations with Morocco. Colonel Joe Starling told Major Schofield to lie low for a few weeks and sent him off to America to do recces for a few weeks until the commotion died down. On his return Major Schofield organised a publicity water jump for British limbless ex-servicemen (Parachute Regiment) Clifford Sadler and Frank Sutton, the Red Devils Team Rigger Albert Hooker (who lost a leg in 1964) and also the inexperienced Sir James Stuart-Monteth who was commissioned into the Scots Guards during WW2. He had lost both his legs from the hip down while serving with the 24th Guards Brigade at Anzio and later became managing director at ICI, generating considerable support to the cause of British servicemen through the organisation BLESMA, British Limbless Ex-servicemen's Association. The team Rigger, Sgt Albert Hooker, designed and made a parachute harness for Sir James to enable him to do the static-line into the Solent where the Royal Marines provided patrol boats and divers to assist when all jumpers landed in the water. He became an inspiration not only to all the young post-Second World War amputees but also to everyone there that day who witnessed him walking on his hands whilst wearing his parachuting equipment to emplane. The event was a major success raising the profile of BLESMA and both Major Schofield and the Red Devils Team were redeemed again in the eyes of the press and the media.

Beaufort Hotel

In 1973 the Team were booked to jump into a parachute display in the Avon town of Bath and were invited to ceremoniously open a newly built hotel. The show organisers had requested both Beauty and the Beast, (me being the beauty and Jim Petherbridge being the beast dressed as Fred, the Gorilla). Jim was one of the tallest members of the team and was also from Bath so he was selected to wear the black, hairy gorilla and also jump the Delta II Parawing parachute which he wasn't overly happy about as it was a particularly hot day. Jim also had to jump in with a big key which was to be used at the opening ceremony when we cut the ribbon and then opened the hotel doors. We flew overhead and had to circle for a while until the orange cross at the rear of the hotel was laid out. It was show time, a low show due to the cloud base being at 1,500ft. I was out first and deployed my Papillon immediately out the door. Jim followed a few seconds later. I watched him pull his ripcord and the red Delta II Para Wing lifted out of his container but the Velcro wrap around the top of the lines remained closed denying the canopy air to inflate it. Jim continued to fall to earth with full line-stretch and a closed canopy, the drag from which put him into a standing up position. Unable to do anything but watch from the security of my own harness, my own canopy fully deployed, I felt totally helpless as Jim grappled in vain to release his Capewell covers, pull the metal rings and release his not-going-to-deploy main parachute. His dark form became a dot in the distance and I thought Jim was going to stoof in big-time but suddenly, just above the trees I saw his red triangular parachute open. Jim was so low he only had time to release his brakes and turn his parachute into wind where he arrived like King Kong doing a nine-yard PLF into the refreshments table at a venue a mile or so short of the hotel. With perfect timing, he stood up then picked up a large teapot that had fallen to the ground with the rest of the table's crockery and cutlery and in his best Bath accent said, "More tea Vicar?" The tranquil setting of tea-sipping guests mulling over life's little eccentricities and swapping cake recipes and life-styles at, co-incidentally, a Vicar's tea party, came to a panicky halt when the women ran screaming while the men picked up chairs to defend themselves. Within minutes a policeman arrived at the scene on his motorbike and Jim hurriedly removed the gorilla head and helmet and while unstrapping his parachute harness apologised profusely to the startled guests explaining he couldn't stay to enjoy the party as he had to dash to open the Beaufort Hotel. He clambered aboard the motorbike, put on his hairy helmet and mask, tucked his parachute firmly under his arm and the policeman drove off in earnest through the streets of Bath where traffic came to a standstill, car drivers rubber necking in disbelief at witnessing a huge, black, hairy gorilla riding pillion. Jim arrived at the entrance to the hotel just in time for the mayor to cut the ribbon and apologised profusely for his late arrival. Jim later elaborated further about his ordeal explaining he couldn't cut-away the streaming Wing canopy due to a number of problems, mainly to do with the long gorilla hair covering the Capewells,while also hindered by the large hairy gloves. His vision through the gorilla mask eye-holes was restricted too and although he could see normally when looking straight ahead, he couldn't see much when looking down or to the side. Lessons were learnt and the following day, the Team Rigger, Sgt Albert Hooker made a number of smooth surfaced waist jackets to wear over the hairy gorilla suit to provide unobstructed access to the Capewells making it easier to take off the dust covers.

With Red Fred (Jim Petherbridge)

1974

In February 1974, after a training camp in Cyprus, the Team took delivery of the first Sleds (square parachute) and began test jumping them on Queens Avenue, Aldershot. Everyone who jumped the Sled, experienced unpredictable and vicious openings and more often than not had to chop it and deploy reserve parachutes. Sgt Bob Harman must go down in the record books for test jumping the Sled and cutting it away. In fact, at one time, Bob had more malfunctions logged than I had jumps and his nickname reflected his persistence trying to crack the opening sequence with different packing methods and even splitting the tail. Bob was known as Captain Marbles for his brave, heroic and derring-do actions which were often reckless but pioneering in developing early square parachutes. It was a period of innovation for the sport and led to unhappy politics between the team and the older members of the BPA who were reluctant to change.

The team were (and still are) completely self-funded, apart from the soldiers on loan from one of the three parent Parachute Regiment Battalions. The equipment we used, team vehicles and training was all funded from the income generated doing parachute displays and training students to skydive.

At the beginning of 1974, we found ourselves without any vehicles as no British Industry could support us with a recession looming. Ford pulled the plug on their offer of vehicles and with a very hectic parachute display season looming, the team's existence was in jeopardy if it couldn't fulfil its obligations to the multitude of show-organisers who had made firm bookings. On one of his mandatory late starts, Major Schofield read his Daily Telegraph and noticed a very bland, full-page Mercedes Benz advert. He immediately dressed and raced to work where he called me and Ted into his office. "I have an idea!" he said, and at that picked up the phone and called Mercedes where he was put through to the Marketing Manager. He announced himself as Major Schofield, Team Commander of The Parachute Regiment Freefall Team, The Red Devils and said, "I think your advertising campaign stinks and I could show you a better way to get Mercedes Benz a lot more publicity than in the Daily Telegraph!" Meanwhile, Ted and I were cringing, open-mouthed with shock at Major Schofield's rudeness as it was so out of character for him. The Marketing Manager however was obviously impressed, told Major Schofield he liked his proposal and asked him to meet, at Mercedes Head Office in Luton, at 12 noon later that day. Major Schofield put down the handset and like a bat out of hell ran out of the Team Room and set off in pursuit of securing some team transport. At the end of the meeting with the Marketing Manager, he'd secured two Mercedes Benz Long Wheelbase Luton Vans to be used carte blanche, the only requirement was that we kept them in pristine condition and they were never to be off the road.

1974 was an excellent competition year for the Red Devils with Scotty Milne, Deak Wright, Dane Kenny and myself making the British Team. I won the National Championships in both Style and Accuracy events and as a Team we won the Team Accuracy Gold and Team Overall Gold qualifying us all to represent the nation at the World Championships in the former eastern-bloc country, Hungary. The other members selected for the British Team were civilians, John Meacock and Tracy Rixon from Peterborough Parachute Centre, the others from Duck End Farm Parachute Club, Bob Hiatt, Bob King, Jane Cain (Waugh), Annie McKie (Swinbourne) with Dougie Peacock as coach and Dave Waugh as Team Leader.

A couple of weeks later, the civilian contingent of the Brit Team travelled to Bad Lippspringe, Germany, for team training prior to the World Meet. Meanwhile, we military bods and Red Devils couldn't attend the training camp immediately as we were scheduled to jump for our boss. On 15th July 1974 Her Majesty Queen Elizabeth II presented the second Colours to all three regular battalions

Sibson Parachute Centre with John Meacock

of The Parachute Regiment and the first colours to the 4th (Volunteer) Battalion. After the ceremonial marches we (the Red Devils) formed a team line-up with the entire Parachute Regiment present and the Queen was introduced to us all individually. When Her Majesty arrived in front of me, Major Schofield said, "This is Sgt Jackie Smith Sir", then quickly corrected himself: "Serving with the Women's Royal Army Corps as a full time member of the Red Devils, Ma'am". Standing proud and to attention before her, she commented on my bravery to jump out of perfectly good airplanes and congratulated me on standing alone in a totally male military environment. Later, I had the honour of attending the Regimental Lunch with the Queen and was due to sit with Major Schofield and his wife, Penny, but such a gentleman that Major Schofield was, he allowed the Mercedes Marketing Manager to have his seat and he sat between Penny and I. It was a totally unselfish gesture on Major Schofield's behalf but the least he could do to thank Mercedes for bailing the team out with such a good sponsorship deal at short notice at the beginning of the busy demo season.

The demo for the Queen's Colours Presentation was the last for Major Schofield and his posting to the team came to an end in early 1975 before leaving the army to return to South Africa in 1976. He kept in touch regularly and said he found it difficult adjusting to civilian life. In 1977 Major Schofield joined the South African Defence Force and served for five years introducing freefall and technical advice on military parachuting. In 1983 he decided to call parachuting a day and nailed his altimeter to the wall in the bar, then returned to his first love, sailing, and found work building catamarans. His life had gone full circle back to his Navy days. Major Schofield always reflected on his time with the Red Devils as the happiest times of his life and held fond memories for him as he truly gave his utmost for the team. At the beginning of 1975 he handed over the Team to Major Gerry O'Hara who assumed the position of Team Commander.

To represent Great Britain at the World Championships the military personnel qualifying had to jump through hoops to obtain special military dispensation to attend, as Hungary was an Eastern-bloc Country behind the Iron Curtain. Our arrival in Hungary caused a commotion of security where everything we carried was scrutinised with a magnifying glass and the host of military and civilian police observed our every move. As military personnel we were identified as potential spies and on the journey from the airport to the World Championships accommodation, police vehicles escorted our bus along with a few military policemen travelling on board with us. The culture shock of being in a communist country was immediately apparent where women had hairy legs and armpits and everyone (it seemed) chain smoked cigarettes. The vehicles on the road were old and dingy and drivers drove fast and aggressively with no consideration for the safety of passengers or those pedestrians trying to cross the road. The shared-sex, foul-smelling and dirty toilets left nothing to the imagination either. Instead of peeing or pooping into water (as we do in the West) the Hungarian design had us doing our business onto a little shelf with about a centimetre of water on top which sat there, fully exposed awaiting a close up inspection. Reaching our temporary accommodation in Szolnok, we were shown our rooms which were dark and squalid with clouds of mosquitoes swarming around, making our lives constantly slap-unhappy and miserable. The following day, we were moved to youth camp which had enormous hot mineral pools, excellent sports facilities and running tracks. The World Championships DZ was flooded and an emergency DZ set up on a military airfield where a 50m sand pit (no gravel) was positioned next to a 100m wide tarmac runway. At the DZ brief we were gob-smacked to be told there was no aerial picture of the DZ and instead a rough pencil drawing of the area was pinned to the wall. We were also advised that as we were on an active military airfield with MIG 15s everywhere, cameras were not allowed, totally banned, with no ground or aerial shots to be taken whatsoever. There were guards and secret police everywhere and not wanting to jeopardise being extracted from the World Meet for the sake of a few photographs, we all abided by the rules and unfortunately came away with very little evidence of having competed there. It was the most testing of accuracy conditions we had ever jumped in, due to the searing heat rising from the sand-pit target area and also the close-by tarmac runway. On one jump in particular, the men's team set up in their stack to approach the pit and changed positions on at least three occasions, the thermals lifting the first and lowest in the stack to be suddenly lifted higher than the top person in the stack.

After the Mercedes sponsorship deal Shell also endorsed the team, providing the team with a healthy fuel package with Shell including clothing which they asked us to wear at all times when on the road and on demos. It was through Shell we took firm bookings every year at all the Formula 1 racetracks which gave us maximum exposure on TV across the globe. Throughout the rest of the year we performed as a team, hundreds of demonstrations jumping into high profile shows including National Horse Racing events and we also did small shows too, donkey derbies, village shows, weddings and even jumped into a few funeral services and scattered someone's ashes in freefall or under the canopy. Scattering someone's ashes into the air is a sombre act but a right and fitting farewell to someone, usually a skydiver, whose wishes are to forever fly free.

1974 – USA Trip

Frustrated by the typical British weather, the persistent rain, low cloud and high winds during a competition at Bridlington drop zone in 1974, we spent our time sitting on parachute packing tables swinging our legs, swigging gallons of tea and generally hanging around waiting to jump. Throughout the bad weather days, we watched American skydiving movies showing blue skies and sunshine, big aircraft and the most awesome skydiving we'd ever seen. It was high on our wish list to experience similar weather conditions ourselves but typically, in the good old British weather, all we could do was talk skydiving and drink beer. We weren't very good at Skydiving but our beer-drinking skills were second to none. Skydivers in America at the time were completing two or three 16-way formations on each jump whereas in Britain the majority of us struggled to get eight people together in a circle (star). There was a wide divide between our weather-hampered skills and those of our American friends across the pond and, keen to improve our own personal flying abilities in a friendlier climate in the USA, we planned a trip to Zephyrhills Parachute Centre, Florida. Every single skydiver on that wet and windy Bridlington drop zone enthusiastically agreed to the adventure but when it actually came to committing to the financial outlay, there were only five of us who went ahead with the plan. Three of the five were full time members of the Red Devils and because we hadn't had any opportunity to take leave or days off (including any weekends) throughout the parachute display season between early March until late October, the team and army allowed one long block leave period for four weeks throughout December. The famous five, (we really were famous for travelling to the USA in those days as very few had done so previously), myself, fellow Red Devils Steve Slater and Dane Kenny, a Royal Corps of Transport skydiving friend Martin 'Togsy' Togher and a REME military friend John 'Wally' Wallace.

We applied for military 'indulgence' flights, (cheap flights in military VC10 aircraft were available to any military personnel on a fill-up basis) and were fortunate to be allocated all five seats together on the same flight. The VC10 flight flew us from RAF Brize Norton, Oxfordshire, to Washington DC, USA, from where we made our way to Zephyrhills Parachute Centre in Florida, flying commercial late night cheap-as-chips stand-by flights. The stand-by flights were subject to availability on a fill-up, first-come-first-served basis for the princely sum of $17 one way. Internal air travel in the States in the early 70s was as easy as catching a bus and after rocking up at an airport and purchasing a ticket, the baggage was checked in without ID or passport check and body security searches were not in existence or even thought about. So simple it was to buy a ticket and board an aircraft in the USA that a few years prior to our trip, an unidentified man approached the airline ticket counter giving his name as Dan B Cooper and purchased a one-way ticket to Seattle. He boarded the Boeing 727 carrying an attaché case, took a seat at the rear of the aircraft, then during mid-flight, he passed a note to the air hostess which she assumed was his telephone number. Without reading the note she slipped it into her purse at which time DB Cooper whispered in her ear, "You'd better look at the note. I have a bomb". He demanded $200,000, four parachutes (two main parachutes and two reserves) and a fuel truck standing by at Seattle airport to refuel the aircraft on arrival. After refuelling and negotiating the ransom money exchange, Cooper directed the pilot to take off again and mid-air between the Oregon-Washington borders, he exited the aircraft, wearing his parachuting equipment, via the rear air-stair which he activated himself.

Our Boeing 727 flight was not quite as eventful as DB Cooper's however but we chatted excitedly about the folklore imagining DB Cooper's experience and what it must have felt like for him to jump from the rear stairs of a commercial passenger jet. The trolley-dollies became understandably concerned as we stood grouped together 'ooing and ahhing' while looking and pointing down the rear stairs. In a firm voice one of the trolley dollies told us to return to our seats immediately so we, being the disciplined soldiers we were, did as we were told, while mumbling "Spoilsport!" under our breaths. We were simply enjoying the moment and had no intention of hijacking the aircraft but the hostess was obviously concerned.

Dane, Steve and I had visited the USA three times previously with the Red Devils, travelling via military connections where we'd trained under the watchful military eye of our hosts, the Golden Knights. The self-organised adventure trip during our Christmas block leave however was totally self-funded and self-organised. Our late-night standby flight landed at Tampa airport and Dane found a public telephone to call the parachute centre and luckily for us the DZ owner, Jim Hooper, said he would send someone to pick us up. We were willing to pay whoever picked us up but such was Jim's hospitality he assured us payment was not necessary but a few cases of beer wouldn't go amiss. Fatigued, smelly and hungry from the long journey, we were at a loss as to where to sleep when we eventually arrived on the drop zone. There were camp fires surrounded by hundreds of beer swilling skydivers who were enthusing, talking loudly (shouting) about their day's skydiving achievements. Individually, they all told incredible stories about their jumps, giving off an impression they were the best skydivers since sliced bread and not holding back letting everyone around them know it. Where we were used to frequenting a warm bar after a day's skydiving drinking pints of beer out of tall glasses, our American compatriots partied, drinking cans of ice cold beers, refrigerated in ice-filled kiddies paddling pools scattered around the drop zone. Music of the era, Pink Floyd, The Eagles, Steve Miller Band, Doobie Brothers, Steely Dan, The Moody Blues and Fleetwood Mac blared loudly from every camper van on the DZ, meanwhile individuals strummed their guitars around camp fires. It was Glastonbury on a Florida DZ.

The partying continued until well into the early hours of the following morning and feeling weary from the day's travel, Dane asked someone if there was anywhere we could lay down our green maggots (army sleeping bags) and sleep for the night. An incredibly friendly and bearded Kevin Shea picked up on Dane's English accent and offered a skydiver's 'cool' thumb-wrapping handshake which looked clumsy and clunky as we conservative Brits had never done one before. Kevin attracted the attention of everyone around by introducing us in a loud voice, "Hey everyone, some Brits are over here for the Boogie. Come and say howdy." In an instant we were surrounded by every skydiver on the drop zone introducing themselves and declaring they had never met a British person or heard an English accent before. They told us it was really neat to hear our cute accents and throughout the night all we heard was them mimicking the way we said "Hello mate" and "Cheers mate". They'd never heard the word 'mate' expressed as 'friend' before. It was totally overwhelming to be in America, on an American drop zone with elite American skydivers we recognised from the movies we'd watched in awe back home in the UK. Kevin asked, "Jeet yet?" and frequently said "FoSho" and we didn't know what he meant. Eventually we realised he was saying "Did you eat yet?" and "for sure" and only then did we confirm we were starving hungry. Kevin drove into Zephyrhills, picked up a half dozen buckets of Kentucky Fried Chicken for us and invited us to join in the party. Kevin was an amazing person and refused to take payment for the KFC chicken or the beers forced down our necks that night and we are forever grateful for his outstanding hospitality and friendship.

The 'beer tents' on the drop zone were old, round parachutes perched onto tall poles creating a shelter from the sun during the day and after inspecting at close range those 'gash' canopies appeared to be in better condition than those we were using to jump with. There were so many surplus military round chutes on the DZ they were ten a penny and really cheap to buy. Z-Hills Parachute centre was hosting the Annual Thanksgiving Turkey Meet and we witnessed more skydivers and aircraft on that DZ than the UK had skydivers in total with about 110 ten-man teams competing. There were also 13 teams competing in a new 20-man star event and with three Dakotas, one Lockheed Loadstar and a few Beech aircraft, about 130 team jumps were made on the first day, with 1,300 descents in total. The pilots were flying so efficiently a 10-man team unloaded from an aircraft at 10,500ft every four and a half minutes. We were gobsmacked having never seen anything like it and the skies were constantly filled with canopies of various colours and shapes. Some were jumping old 'cheapos' TU and LL canopies which were short-lined with apexes pulled down and we were introduced to Strato-Stars, Piglet 1s and 2s and also the Wonder Hog container. The skydivers at the Turkey Meet generally had long flowing hair and wore either sweat bands or brightly coloured bandanas over their heads; meanwhile Dane, Steve, Togsy and Wally looked decidedly out of place, sticking out like sore thumbs, with their military clean-cut, short back and sides hairstyles. Everyone wore voluminous jumpsuits made out of heavy canvas or thick cotton material and the sleeves and legs were patterned with psychedelic designs, flowers and skydiving patches, XX, 24, 16, SCR, SCS they had achieved. Some jumpsuits had more underarm 'wing' material than my parachute was big, (ok, I exaggerate for effect) and seemingly the bigger the wing, the cooler the skydiver looked. Later, on our return to the UK, we copied the size of jumpsuit but not necessarily the professional design and style, by lying down on Army mattress covers which were made out of heavy canvas and cut around to make huge suits that made us fly, not like eagles, but like turkeys and out of control manifest boards.

After a few days at Z-Hills, we decided to drive south in a skydiving friend's camper van to Poppenhager's parachute centre located further south and just outside Indiantown. We arrived at the drop zone late in the evening and everything was locked up, so laid our green maggots on the grass next to the parachute centre's bunkhouse walls. Sleep evaded us because we couldn't stop talking about the size of the moon, so big it looked close enough to touch and not only was it large but so bright we felt like we were in the full glare of a giant spotlight. Throughout the night, we just laid in our green maggots talking and watching the night sky which was an explosion of shooting stars unlike anything we'd ever seen before. The sandman eventually caught up with us however, but sleep was short-lived due the familiar sound of a log being sawn with a chainsaw. It was of course, Togsy snoring and no matter what position he laid in, the snoring continued on both the inhale and exhale. The first person to arrive at the DZ was a chap called Paul but we didn't connect his first name to the 'Poppenhager' person we'd heard about. In a laid-back and casual way, he introduced himself as our pilot for the day then told us he was going for breakfast and asked did we need a ride too? It was late morning and the weather conditions were perfect with tantalizingly blue skies and light winds and we were chomping at the bit to jump but without the pilot we couldn't get airborne. We had no choice but to tag along with him into Indiantown where we over-indulged on the biggest breakfasts known to man. Eggs over easy, crispy bacon, hash browns, grits, pancakes and syrup, a huge selection of toast all washed down with bottomless cups of coffee. I was so uncomfortably bloated, my belly protruding like that of a snake after swallowing a sheep and later on the DZ, I could barely bend over to pick up my equipment. Aboard the Cessna aircraft on jump run Togsy, our jump master, gave some flight corrections to Paul who casually shook his head declining any change in the aircraft's flight path towards the exit point. Togsy became increasingly agitated and thankfully his barrage of abuse was both lost in translation and drowned out by the aircraft's noisy engines. Paul eventually gave in to Togsy's flight corrections and steered the aircraft into a radical 45 degree turn, so radical we nearly fell out the door and seconds later Togsy gave us the thumbs up to climb out. At last, we were jumping in America. The yahooing however, came to an abrupt halt when we realised how strong the upper winds were and as we sailed backwards over the drop zone, we then each had to negotiate a safe landing area amongst the power cables, orange groves and surrounding water canals. Once on the ground we negotiated either a long walk or cross through the water in the deep canal but it became evident the latter wasn't an option as the logs we thought were just logs floating on the surface were actually alligators. We'd have been eaten alive!

Later that day we discovered that Paul, our pilot, was in fact the sky-god that is 'Pop' Poppenhager. He'd made his first jump, a military jump prior to the Korean war at the age of 19 and as part of the 82nd Airborne Division he became a military parachute rigger, test jumper and trained both military personnel and civilians. It was quite humbling knowing we'd assumed he was 'just' the pilot when he flew us on that first lift and I learned from then on never to make assumptions of anyone, not just in skydiving but in life! From then on we sat back and enjoyed the watery and scenic Florida views, trusting Pop's flying skills and territorial knowledge until he cut the engines for us to exit. On one particular jump, we left the aircraft and in the slipstream Togsy became very animated, his face in shock and he was frantically pointing to something below us. An airline passenger jet, possibly a Boeing 727, was directly underneath us and so near we deployed our parachutes immediately. After three days at Pop's place, we decided to travel to Deland Parachute Centre with some friends who'd offered us a lift in their motor home. Deland flew a Dakota DC3 jump aircraft and we met a multitude of skydivers who were all too eager to jump with us as most had never met a 'real live Brit' before. The DZ was very basic with no facilities apart from one toilet in the hangar and no snack-bar. We went hungry for three days and slept sitting upright on tatty commercial airline seats in the hangar, the seats unfortunately unable to recline but at least we had a roof over our heads in the torrential storm that crashed and banged like WW3 outside. It was at Deland we chanced across a super chap by the name of Paul McCowan who, whilst packing his parachute expressed his intentions to drive across to Casa Grande and do some jumping at 'The Gulch'. We'd read about the drop zone Paul referred to in the parachuting magazines *RW Underground* and *Spotter* and at that DZ the United States Freefall Exhibition Team (USFET), the cream of the worldwide skydiving crop, performed innovative skydiving formations on a daily basis. It was the USFET who featured in the skydiving movies we'd watched over and over again during our weathered-out down time at Bridlington that had inspired us to travel to the USA in the first place. The word on the street regarding The Gulch's reputation however was something to behold with a 'Sport Death' reputation, its logo image of a sun-dried withered arm and hand perched aloft on a pole. Skydiving folklore had it that the arm had been found in the desert and belonged to a skydiver, but as the prop turns, so do stories. Paul was keen to skydive with us and asked if we would like to accompany him in his red camper van on the long journey, 2,074 miles to Arizona. Looking at the distance on the paper road map didn't appear to be far but in reality the actual journey took nearly three days of non-stop driving, passing west out of Florida to Tallahassee and Pensacola on State International 10 through the states of Alabama, Mississippi and Louisiana. The maximum speed limit across the United States was 55mph and the only time we exceeded that was when we tailgated lorries in long convoys, the drivers alerting each to the whereabouts of Smokey (police) via Citizens Band radio. The radios were crucial for independent truckers; many were paid by the mile, which meant their productivity was impacted by the slow speed limit. At the Texas border control we had to declare the food we'd stashed on board Paul's camper van, as fruit and vegetables are carefully monitored in America to prohibit the introduction of agricultural pests and diseases. Before departing Florida we'd loaded up with bags of cheap oranges to eat on the journey and border control instructed us to ditch the fruit in the bins before crossing the state line. To us Brits, throwing the fruit away was sacrilege so we decided to eat the lot rather than leave it to waste and much to the amusement of the border control staff and others in passing vehicles, we stood on the roadside peeling oranges stuffing as many as we could into our mouths. The journey through Texas was bum-squaringly long, the road never-ending and the same distance as from John O'Groats to Land's End. We watched the sun rise, the sun set, and the sun rise again and it was with such relief to cross the Arizona state line and make our way to the DZ. The DZ was closed and a few skydivers invited us to join them for a meal in a local restaurant where Paul ordered rib-eye steaks for everyone. I might be exaggerating, like I do, for effect but my potato was the size of a rugby ball and because I hadn't eaten much on the long road journey, I woofed it down with shedloads of butter and sour cream, and not forgetting the 161 items I'd picked from the salad bar too. My tummy was about to burst when the waitress arrived with a rib-eye steak and placed it on the table under my nose. It was bigger than any roast beef joint my entire family shared for Sunday lunch and I couldn't believe it was all for me. Everyone tucked into what must have been an entire cow and not a morsel was left on anyone's plate. I can't begin to tell you how uncomfortable we were, our bellies bloated so much we could barely move and for the following two days we groaned, resembling Godzillas in jumpsuits, the zips on the verge of busting open and no-one able to bend over to pick up the equipment.

Casa Grande was THE place to be for progressive skydiving and each day we watched in awe as those sky-gods we'd watched in the movies were performing before our very eyes, the skies above were filled with 16 man formations. Throughout the following weeks, we skydived our butts off doing some amazing stuff and ultimately jumping with the USFET to achieve our 8 and then 16-man patches. I'd borrowed BJ Worth's white USFET jumpsuit for some of my latter skydives and truly believed it was his suit that flew me into the large formations and so impressed, I ordered one as soon as my feet hit the ground.

There was no accommodation on the DZ but every night we were invited to a party at someone's house and made welcome to find floor space to sleep overnight. The only floor space to be found at one of the parties was a small broom cupboard which Steve Slater and myself squeezed into, our heads touching one wall, toes touching the other. Meanwhile the party continued throughout the night and we didn't get a wink of sleep, laughing at some of the noises coming from the adjoining bedroom. It was the best sex I never had and whoever was making the noises had a really good time.

At the weekends, small competitions took place with 10-man teams galore turning up. One of the, shall we say, characterful 'crazy' jumpers on the DZ was Scotty Carbone who was so much fun and larger than life. Everyone who had the fortune to cross his path had a story to tell about him. He was one of a kind, the king of party, charming, funny, outrageously loud, over the top flamboyant and exceptionally defiant, freefalling down to heights of around 400ft before deploying his Piglet 2 round parachute, resulting in him being grounded on more than one occasion but he never missed an opportunity to make a fast buck and set up a very popular DZ snack-bar selling bounce-burgers and Egglet II rolls.

It was at The Gulch we saw parachuting equipment modified to make it lighter and therefore more trendy. Old C9LL and TU canopies were short-lined and gutted of their inner strands reducing the packing volume, weight and obviously tensile strength and surprisingly never witnessed any line breakage throughout the four weeks on the DZ. It was the dawn of a new era in lighter gear and another step away from surplus military equipment which the majority of skydivers used then.

Paul was jumping a red Jump Shack Racer with a Red Strato-Star as his main parachute and everyone on the DZ was intrigued at how small and compact the container was compared to the old B4 backpacks everyone else was still jumping. It was there we jumped our first Strato-Star canopies and were so impressed all five of us purchased Racers from Sandy Reid's mobile shop on the DZ.

It was home time and our return journey from Phoenix to Washington DC was one of short hops on cheap standby night flights. We were exhausted and smelly from carrying our heavy para bags through the capital and all I wanted to do was soak in a bath, have a meal and slip between the sheets of my bed. The boys however, perked up considerably when they heard Deep Throat was showing in a cinema close by and took the opportunity to watch the first of its kind pornographic film as it had been banned in the UK. I slept like a baby and was awakened by the female member of staff at the hostel who had booked us in the previous night. She'd laundered all my smelly clothing laying out my jeans, t-shirt and underwear next to my bed and wouldn't accept any payment for doing so. I smelled as fresh as a daisy on the return flight to UK, unlike the blokes who had sacrificed the opportunity of an early night and freshly laundered clothes by going out to the cinema. I doubt very much they were bothered too much however as they slept the entire journey no doubt dreaming of Linda Lovelace's G-spot which the blokes informed me was in the back of her throat. Dream on lads!

1975 & 76

As part of the competition team we also competed in every meet in the UK with huge success at the European Championships in Schaffen, Belgium. At the Army Parachuting Championships, we (The Red Devils) swept the board taking every trophy in each event. Following on from the Armies, we then took gold in most events in the UK, Shobdon, Peterborough, Duck End Farm, then at the National Championships in all the individual events, taking 1st Place in Team Accuracy and Team Overall. At the Rhine Army Championships in Germany we also swept the board as a team with Dicky, Deak and Scotty performing really well. Disappointingly, on my last accuracy jump my canopy stopped dead on approach, lifted up into the sky by a thermal and then slammed me unceremoniously into the pea-gravel where I scored 47 centimetres. "Shit!" That one jump took me from 1st place overall into fourth place overall, but I still took gold in the lady's event. Competition is all about winning and losing. There is the thrill of victory then the agony of defeat and experiencing the emotions of both is all part of the lesson. To lose IS the lesson. Learn from it, pick yourself up off the floor, get on with it and remember the lesson. I'd never say however, that it didn't matter to me if I lost as I entered every competition positively with the intention of winning.

Competition Team

It was a great ending to an incredibly busy, productive and successful year on The Red Devils team and with our public profile increasing, the Team were offered fantastic sponsorship deals by many large corporations recognising enormous media exposure for their brands.

1976 also proved to be an even busier demo season with over 350 shows booked, regular passing out parade demos into Browning Barracks, performing at every Army Show and air display around the country and then the additional late bookings into weddings or the occasional funeral. We also, as a team, had excellent competition results in all the regional meets around the country and again wiped the board at the Army and National Championships winning gold in just about every event. It was at the Rhine Army Championships in Germany I first dead-centred a competition out, scoring 0.00 on every jump and taking 1st place overall individually and also in the team events. The Red Devils were invited to jump into the prize-giving event after the competition ended and eight of us did a team stack, taking bets in the aircraft on the way up to jump altitude, the loser to buy the beers. Although the competition had ended we continued, as always, to compete against each other on each and every jump. As top person in the stack, I'd no idea what anyone else had scored and set up on my final approach. The silence was deafening and every set of eyes was watching my descent until I planted the disc with my heel. All eight of us scored a dead-centre and so it was party-party time. Did we celebrate that night? Did we ever!

At the RAPA meet there was only one shower block, so separate male and female timed sessions were posted at the manifest for everyone to see. It didn't work out that you could shower during the allocated session however, due to the jumping programme not fitting with the timings and everyone showered whenever there was an opportunity between jumps. On each occasion I visited the shower block, I stripped off discretely before stepping into the shower and closed the curtain assuming I was secure in the confines of my cubicle space. In the bar one evening, a chap I didn't know very well approached and offered to buy me drink. It would have been rude to decline such a kind gesture so I accepted and as he handed the large glass of wine to me, I asked why he'd bought it for me. There was me thinking he was going to chat me up but instead he burst out laughing, telling me I'd made his day when I'd bent over in the shower to pick up the soap! I nearly choked and the large mouthful of wine I'd just swigged from the glass spurted out all over him! That'll teach him to be a peeping Tom!

In November, when the demo season ended, we took off again on our annual jolly across the pond in the US of A to train and compete with the Golden Knights at Laurinburg, St Mère Église, Raeford, Louisburg, Barnwell jumping out of C130s in crystal clear blue skies. There were no round canopies on this trip, everyone was either on Strato-Stars or Wing, Sled, ParaPlane and thankfully no more downwind landings into the pit for accuracy. How skydivers survived those downwind accuracy landings for so long, especially in marginal competition winds I will never know. Landing, or should I say arriving, in the pea gravel on windy days was like doing combat with the ground. On some of the hard and fast landings I'm sure I shifted the pit 50 metres further downwind and afterwards retrieved pea-gravel from every orifice, and I mean EVERY orifice! The square parachute into-wind landings were so much gentler on our knees and our bodies took fewer knocks reducing our injuries tenfold.

The last day of jumping at Laurinburg, 26th November, proved to be an historic moment for the Team when we built the Red Devils' first 8 and then 9-man star with Golden Knight's aerial photographer, Bill Wenger, docking 10th. We were so excited we screamed and yahooed, holding the formation for what seemed forever, nearly funnelling when everyone celebrated by thrashing and kicking their legs in freefall. We landed off the DZ but didn't care one iota. The whole world is a DZ at epic times like that. There was no disputing who was getting the beers in for that 'first' and later in the bar, we stunned the barman with our drinking skills. The only reason we went to our beds that night was because we drank the bar dry. For the record, the individuals on the skydive were Dougie Young, Deak Wright, Dane Kenny, Dicky (Martin) Bird, Steve Eversfield, Chris Simpson, Andy Sinclair, Steve Slater, me and Bill Wenger.

Unfortunately, Scotty, who should have been on the load, missed the day's skydiving due to illness so it was a pretty miserable night for him watching us celebrating and getting drunk later that evening in the bar.

Team Line-up

During the '76 season I had the opportunity to meet an amazing lady, my absolute heroine who appears to have slipped through the cracks in history. Her name is Dolly Shepherd and when she flew with us and watched us jump, said she wished she hadn't been born so soon. Her parachuting career dates from the beginning of the 20th century when her sport was enjoyed by only a handful of men and women. The harnesses being used today didn't exist in her day and the only link she had with the parachute was a trapeze bar to which she had to cling onto. Dolly was one of a team of eight, four men and four women who toured the country giving parachute displays. Her parachute was stretched out on the ground with pleats and lines neatly arranged. The top of the canopy was then attached under the balloon and at the bottom of the canopy's lines was a trapeze bar which Dolly had to clasp firmly. A loose sling of webbing passed between her legs to help take the weight of her body. A gas filled balloon was held down with sandbags until it was time for lift off and in the case of the hot air balloon, the envelope was held over a fire pit by about twenty-four sturdy men until it was filled and ready to lift. There was no propane gas in those days. Dolly had to let go of the trapeze bar at around 4,000ft when she'd pull the ripcord and her canopy fell away from the balloon for about 250ft before opening. With no steering lines on her canopy she never landed in the area she'd ascended from and occasionally made some hairy landings on rooftops and trees. On one occasion both the balloon and the parachute malfunctioned and she found herself rising to 15,000ft where the cold and lack of oxygen threatened to make her lose her grip and fall to her death. Fortunately, the balloon returned to earth with Dolly still holding onto the trapeze. In a later incident, Dolly ascended with another lady whose parachute would not release from the balloon so Dolly held onto her and they both descended under one parachute. The rate of descent was very fast and Dolly sustained serious injuries and was paralysed for a long time, but eventually recovered to return to her passion for parachuting. When we were introduced, Dolly shook my hand and nearly crushed my knuckles with her amazingly strong grip. Unfortunately, after exchanging stories briefly, I had to pack my parachute to prepare for another show at a different location and we said our goodbyes. What amazes me more about her incredible story is the fact she had to wear a long dress to perform the stunts, as females were not allowed to wear trousers in that era. Skydiving has come a long way in the 100 years since Dolly was parachuting and it was an incredible honour to meet her and her family.

The 1976 National Championships took place at Shobdon Airfield in Hereford where 58 competitors attended all hoping to make the British Team selection. The skydiving population lived under canvas and with no basic toilet or washing facilities available, as the days went on it became pretty grim as far as hygiene was concerned, so we took to the nearby river and bathed in the freezing cold water.

Competitors made their way to the circle of haystacks situated by the landing pit area for pre-competition briefing. At the briefings, the judges and pilots make aware safety points and local farmer rules highlighting the procedure for the competition and also draw numbers out of a hat deciding competitors' jump sequence. Everyone was seated either on the ground or on the haystacks and the only person missing was Gerry McAuley who was to pilot the Cessna 172 during the competition. Gerry, a Canadian, is a fun guy to be around and is always smiling and telling jokes. As he approached his space on the haystack, we noticed he was limping and walking with what looked like an injured ankle. He sat on the haystack and crossed one leg over the other placing his foot on his thigh, the arch of his shoe pointing upwards. He began talking about the aircraft and safety when someone pointed to his shoe and shouted, "Yeeeeeew! Gerry you have dog shit on your shoe". What looked like the biggest dollop of dog doo I have ever witnessed didn't faze Gerry one bit and he calmly scraped his index finger under the mess, smelled it, then put it in his mouth to eat. Everyone fell about gagging, balking and retching disgusted that Gerry had eaten the mess and it wasn't until a short while later he told us he had purchased a new pair of trainers earlier that afternoon in Hereford and plastered crunchy peanut butter onto the shoe's arch. What a laugh!

Two competitors who were in contention for British Team selection were Bobby Hull and Tony Uragallo who'd shown excellent form in numerous competitions earlier that year, but unfortunately didn't make the cut. Over ten rounds of accuracy, Bobby Hull scored 9 x 0.00cm and on one jump 0.02cm giving a 2cm total making him a very worthy National Accuracy Champion. Bobby didn't compete in the Style event and unfortunately British Team selection was the overall placings in both to qualify. Tony Uragallo was in amazing form too and scored 9 x 0.00 and dropped short scoring a catastrophic zap, 10 metres, on one jump dashing any consideration for selection. I can still remember him crying out, "Oh no! Oh no!" as he approached the pit in the knowledge he was dropping short. It was a huge disappointment that day for him and everyone around the pit watching. The BPA competitions sub-committee discussed taking both Bobby and Tony to the British Team's training camp where the best of the selected individuals could show their true worth, but the decision was voted 6-4 against the idea. Both Bobby and Tony would have been potential medal winners at the World Championships but never given the opportunity. In my eyes, Bobby Hull should have certainly been allowed a place on the British Team as National Champion but was declined the opportunity.

Scotty, Dicky, and myself were selected from our National Championships placings to represent Great Britain again, this time at the World Championships in Guidonia, Italy. The men's team should have included John Meacock but he declined his place for business reasons. The Team without John was made up of Scotty Milne, Dicky Bird, Robin Mills, Ken Mapplebeck, Bob Hiatt and Bob King. The ladies team consisted of Sally Smith, Jane Waugh, Chris McGuire, Sandy Murray and myself, with Doug Peacock and Charlie Shea-Simonds as head of delegation and judge. No British company came forward to sponsor our team but BPA Secretary General, Bill Paul secured a fabulous deal with Fiat, an Italian motor company, supplying us with four vehicles. With all four vehicles loaded up with parachuting gear and personal clothing, we drove to our training camp at Bergerac in the beautiful Dordogne region of France, where the skydiving legend, Monsieur Michel Prik hosted and coached us for a couple of weeks. Flying to altitude over Bergerac gave us a bird's eye view of a most beautiful region flying over châteaux, surrounding vineyards and ancient medieval villages. They say beauty is in the eyes of the beholder and I consider myself so lucky to have had the opportunity to see such scenic views all over the world, from aloft, in pursuit of my skydiving hobby.

Ladies British Team 1976

After the training camp we faced the long 1500km road journey to the World Championships which were to take place in Guidonia, an airfield some ten miles outside Rome. We took the scenic coastal route via Montpellier, Marseille, Cannes, Nice and eventually Monaco where we stopped overnight at a friend's house, all sleeping on the living room floor. Refreshed from our overnight rest and quick dip in the Mediterranean Sea at Monte Carlo, we pushed on for the final leg and drove solid for another eight hours before reaching our World Championships destination of Guidonia. We all performed really well at the championships where most competitors were jumping square parachutes. Bob Hiatt, representing Great Britain, scored 0.00cm on each of his first six jumps and then had a bad foot placement scoring 4cm, then 1cm on his 7th and 8th jump, missing out on a bronze medal by a measly 1cm. So close, but oh so far away! It was at that World Championships I witnessed the first person to score dead-centres on each of the eight accuracy jumps, with Jean Dermine of France lifting the bar higher for the following World Championships two years later in 1978, where the accuracy event became ten rounds rather than eight and the use of electronic scoring.

At the beginning of 1977, I decided to say goodbye to the military, leaving behind me the Red Devils Team, as I wanted to pursue more competition in Relative Work, an event dominated by civilian teams worldwide. It was a monumental decision to leave such an established military team but the pull of competition without military obligations and endless road journeys after jumping into show grounds, proved too inviting. The new kids on the competition block, Symbiosis, were the rising stars in British Relative Work and had an upcoming training camp in Spring 1977 at Pope Valley, California. With Dane, who had left the military in 1976 to become a professional under-water diver, we joined the British skydiver migration to warmer climes to jump and train alongside the sport's cream of the crop, USA World Champions, Mirror Image. Up until that training camp, no-one in the world had used in-air video and it was Symbiosis (William Grut) who invested in a Polavision system mounted on a cameraman's helmet (mine for the four-way), the in-air jump captured on VHS. This system proved interesting, especially travelling with a huge TV on the journey from Heathrow to Pope Valley and many questioned, "Why are you taking a TV with you?" Polavision gave results a few minutes after landing. The films were very expensive, the quality appalling, but nevertheless a futuristic training aid. Before Polavision, teams such as Mirror Image took films captured in-air (some by cameraman Dave Waterman) into San Francisco for processing and got it back a couple of days later. The films provided the best training aid for teams and also Saturday night's entertainment in Pope Valley's bar where everyone gathered around watching World Champions in the making. Within a very short time afterwards came the demise of VHS and old fashioned tube cameras, and relative work was no longer judged by ground-to-air video but rather, as today, by air-to-air footage.

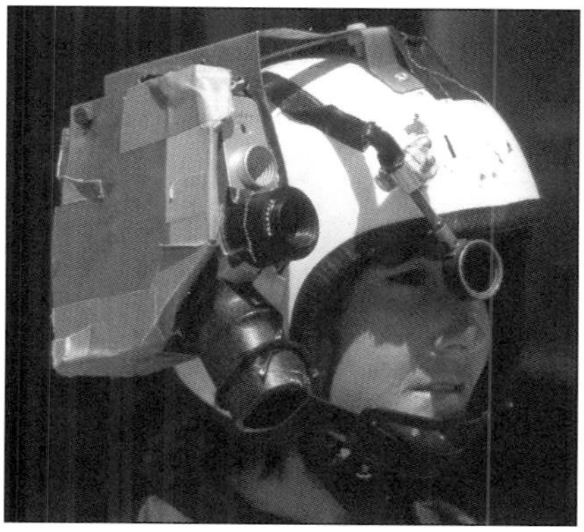
Wearing the Polavision Camera
with Newton Ringsight

Pope Valley

In the mid-70s what was once Usibelli's airfield and restaurant, became Pope Valley Parachute Ranch owned and managed by two US National Parachute Team members, Curt Curtis and Tim Saltenstall. During a parachute meet at Lakehurst in 1969, Tim and Curt began talking about setting up a first-class DZ, patterned on the ski resort theme with all the amenities, bar, restaurant, swimming pool, motel, a clean operational hangar, classroom, training area, good student equipment, multiple aircraft, experienced jump pilots, riggers, instructors and jump-masters. Curt and Tim knew it had to be a 12-month a year operation with good weather which led them to consider Florida, Arizona, Southern California and Northern California. There were other locations which could fulfil the criteria but Florida and California were the main places where they thought the skydiving resort should be. After studying the weather in both locations, it was confirmed it had to be California and in 1970, Curt and his wife, Annie, moved to Monterey, CA where he took a job as Assistant Executive Director of United States Parachute Association. Annie had been a member of the Calistoga Skydivers (next valley over) and had observed the Pope Valley set-up and airstrip while climbing to altitude and thought it was worth looking into. Tim Saltenstall travelled to California to check out Pope Valley as the chosen location and had the same reaction as everyone else: perfect!!

Curt and Tim flew to Alaska to initiate negotiations with Joe Usibelli (the landowner) and after some toing and froing, secured a deal. Curt and Tim took over Pope Valley airstrip in January 1972 and opened with a very limited schedule as they were still acquiring aircraft, pea gravel, and the right people to staff the operation. Pope Valley became known as the Mecca of skydiving after inviting Chris Needels, Commanding Officer of the Golden Knights, to take his competition team for the first big style and accuracy meet, enhancing the reputation as an all-around skydiving operation. Pope Valley was already established with Relative Work team jumping with United States national team caliber competition teams (PB&J, Northstar) training there, as well as Jim Crocker and his British Team, Endrust, and the Gullycats from Australia. Curt was no stranger to competition himself and was Team Leader for both the 1971 Team (Pan Am Cup, Tequesquitengo, Mexico) and the 1972 Team (Tahlequah, Oklahoma, USA). Curt picked up a four-man team, 'Team Up', at the World Cup in Oudtshoorn, South Africa with other sky-gods, BJ Worth, Mike Gennis and Dave Singer. Sitting comfortably in second place and close on the heels of the leaders, Team Up were told that due to the competition being far behind schedule, only flag carrying teams (rather than scratch teams) could continue in the competition, so their world status challenge came abruptly to an end. In 1977 Curt was a member of the legendary Mirror Image 8-way team, winning the United States National Championships then further excelled in winning gold at the World Championships (8-way) in Gatton, Australia. In essence, Pope Valley and the people who jumped there were simply the best in the world, it really was the Mecca of skydiving.

The journey to the DZ took us north out of San Francisco across the Golden Gate Bridge and up the winding roads leading into canyons and Napa valleys on Route 29 through Yountville and St Helena. North of St Helena the road bears right into Deer Park and from there on the road winds and wends its way to Angwin. Angwin is a small town populated by a large community of Seventh Day Adventists and is the closest town, some ten miles or so, from Pope Valley. Stopping at Angwin to stock up on food and essentials, we were made very much aware of the community's religious beliefs when we asked at the local supermarket where the beer and wine section was. They didn't sell alcohol and neither did anyone in the entire town. What we did purchase however was loads of fruit, healthy snacks, grains, carob chocolate which become the main ingredients of our drop zone day-time grazing.

For a few weeks each spring, Pope Valley is carpeted in green and sprinkled with thousands upon thousands of wild flowers, and bordering Pope Valley is the beautiful Lake Berryessa which is the largest lake in Napa County; its reservoir is formed by the Monticello Dam which provides the water to the North Bay region of San Francisco Bay Area. Besides being a haven for skydivers, it was also a cyclist's paradise – the entire valley was flat, cool and breathtakingly beautiful. As a skydiving team we weren't there to pick flowers or cycle; we had lots of skydiving training to keep us busy, our intention was to jump from dawn to dusk every single day, in the more-or-less-guaranteed wall-to-wall blue skies. Pope Valley is a mass of vineyards and apart from a small garage and quaint store where the owner kept his collection of rattlesnakes and short lengths of razor wire, the only other tourist attraction in the vicinity is Litto's Hubcap Ranch which boasts Guinness Book of World Records status. Only in Pope Valley could one man's fetish for hubcaps become a nationally recognised work of art.

In later years, Ernie Butler and Tom Piras managed the bar and restaurant while Canadian 'Kanuk' Dave Wagner managed the kitchen. All three were recognisably talented skydivers who spent what time they could skydiving during the day and never failing to prepare and provide a 'mass' gourmet meal each evening for the hungry skydiving community. The drop zone was so remote the restaurant and bar was packed to the rafters at the end of each day, but not everyone had enough money to eat, drink and skydive. Those with enough money set aside for food, sat at long wooden tables while tucking into their evening meals which was usually the only meal of the day. Those who couldn't afford to eat, the 'lurkers', sat around the edges of the room like hungry wolves, their mouths watering while eyeing every forkful of food lifted from plate to mouth. If anyone stood up to leave the table, the lurkers raced to pick up the plate, eat the left-overs and lick the plate clean and shiny. On numerous occasions when new and first timers arrived on the DZ, they made the mistake of placing their meal on the table, then return to the serving hatch for condiments or napkins only to return to a half empty plate. The rule of thumb when eating a meal at Pope Valley was to guard it with your life, never leave it unattended and never fall into the trap of glancing away when some trickster pointed and commented, "Look at that!" Even while eating your food you had to be on guard, cowering over the plate and ready to deflect any incoming forks.

The DZ's motel accommodation, 'Hotel California', was luxury for those who could afford to rent a room. Each large room had four bunk beds, showers, loo facilities and air conditioning which was a must in the hot and balmy Californian climate. Outside the restaurant was a welcoming swimming pool in which to cool down or practice aircraft exits from a mock-up Beech aircraft door at the deep end. Becky Livingstone and her dog, Indigo, managed the DZ and her office looked out towards the single tarmac airstrip and hangar, where the drop zone's jump ships, DC3, Beech 18 Aircraft and Cessna 182 were parked. There was only one word to describe Pope Valley, idyllic!

To save money for skydiving, I elected to live in 'Chez Tent' rather than move into 'Hotel California' and pitched on the airfield side of the swimming pool fence, where from my tent door, I looked out into the wilderness beyond. As the moon rose into the night sky, the haunting howls of a lone coyote pierced the air triggering echoing replies from tent city dwellers of the human kind, howling long into the night. Dawn was a chorus of opening door zippers and rapid half-naked exits escaping the heat searing through the tent skin. The view each morning from outside my tent door was like a magical mystical dream, the wispy mist tumbling down the Potts Peak's slopes, before magically evaporating into thin air when it reached the warmth of the valley floor. What better way to start the day with a burst of morning glory before the hustle and bustle of each training day.

Removed from the normal rigours of the nine-to-five regime, my drop zone days were blissfully free of regulations. I preferred not to wear a wrist watch throughout training as my daily routine was simple; watch the sunrise, run, eat, shower, jump, pack, jump, pack, jump, pack, jump, pack, watch the sunset from aloft on the sunset load, land, kick back and lie on my unpacked parachute, absorb the day's vibes and watch the fading day darken into night. Free from pollution of ambient light, the Pope Valley night skies became a sea of stars twinkling like jewels. Time for a beer, shower, eat and more beer.

Enjoying the Pope Valley sunshine

The first lift of the day was flown, usually, by Rande De Luca, a member of the United States Freefall Exhibition Team (and later Mirror Image) who had revolutionised skydiving in the early 70s. I'd met Rande in 1974 when our paths crossed at the Gulch, Casa Grande, and it was a great pleasure to fly with such an incredibly talented pilot, skydiver and in-air photographer again. The first time he flew us Brits we sat on board the Cessna aircraft and Rande shouted at the top of his voice, "Get outta the way" which made us Brits laugh out loud. It was a far cry from the stiff upper lipped and very British 'Chocks away' and 'Stand clear' we were used to. Sitting in the open doorway while climbing to altitude was in itself a magical experience, looking out over the Napa Valley's vineyards, its undulating countryside and further in the distance to San Francisco, where a blanket of white, thick fog lingered over the distinguishing feature of the Golden Gate Bridge majestically poking out of the top.

A memorable jump for me at Pope Valley was out of Norton Thomas's Great Lakes aircraft. He climbed the aircraft to 7,000ft and when overhead the drop zone, he dived the aircraft at the ground with great speed. He pulled back the joystick and in an instant felt the G force pressing me hard into my seat before the aircraft went into a tall loop. Inverted and looking at blue fields and green skies, I gently pushed against the seat and popped out of the aircraft where I watched Norton continue on the line of flight, upside down.

As a team, we occasionally made the unanimous decision to take a day off from skydiving, breather days, to restore a balance of normality away from the tensions of living in each other's pockets 24/7. While some ventured off to visit one of the many surrounding vineyards sipping and sampling fine wines, the rest of us soaked in the outdoor hot mineral springs at Calistoga, taking in some of the local sights including 'Old Smoky' geyser. Some ventured into the 7th Day Adventist town of Angwin to empty their minds and stare aimlessly at spinning tumble dryers at the local launderette. On 'breather' days I cycled the fifteen or so miles to Lake Berryessa. Turning right out of Pope Valley Parachute Ranch onto Pope Canyon Road onto desolate roads passing creeks and canyons where apart from a few vultures sitting at the river's edge waiting for a tasty white British bird, I was completely alone not meeting or seeing another person or vehicle on the entire journey.

The skydiving community at Pope Valley were the cream of the crop with the top teams in every event training there. It was the local drop zone for Mirror Image who were the unbeatable US National 8-way and World Champions. A host of international teams and individuals trained at Pope too, Canadians, Aussies, Kiwis, Swedes, Norwegians, Dutch, Germans and Brits and most of the fun-jumping, away from training jumps, were of the highest quality. It was easy to pick up a fun bunch for the sunset 'loose' load where we regularly achieved 16, 20 or 25-way formation skydives with minimal ground organisation or dirt-diving. The drop zone was filled with so much world class talent and refreshingly there was not the slightest whiff of politics or ego.

Pope Valley Parachute Ranch

Symbiosis

Competitions in 1977 started well for Symbiosis where we won the National Championships Accuracy event (Dane Kenny, Robin Mills, Tony Uragallo and myself) winning the team accuracy, the overall team title (in style and accuracy) and me winning both the style and accuracy ladies events. A few months later, Symbiosis also took first place in both the 4 and 8-way at the Relative Work National Championships, but the BPA council decided our team could only participate in one event at the World Championships in Australia. We chose to go to Australia as the British 8-man team, the runners-up in the 4-man events were the RAFSPA team from Weston on the Green and therefore selected to go to the World Championships too. Military service commitments prevented them joining us on concentrated training camps in Bergerac but later joined us in Lyon, where we trained out of the Twin Otter aircraft, giving us the opportunity to get used to the same aircraft being used at the World Championships. It was really interesting being in the aircraft watching the RAF team's exits when they

British 8-way Team – Gatton, Australia

tested the pilot's flying skills with their energetic, "Ready! Ready! Three, Two, One, GO!" countdown while jumping up and down in unison in the open doorway, their combined weight rocking the tail up and down so violently the aircraft nearly stalled while the pilot fought to control it.

In late October both teams set off for Sydney on the inaugural Malaysian Airline System DC10 Flight where we languished in luxury, drinking free booze until we arrived at Kuala Lumpur. We witnessed the most amazing electrical storm, the torrential rain drenching us to the skin, quickly sobering us up when we made our way down the steps from the aircraft and raced across the pan to the terminal. Reaching Australia, we travelled north to Ramblers Drop Zone in Caloundra, Brisbane, where we found basic facilities with just a club hut, a couple of marquees, a grass strip covered in grazing kangaroos and tons of kangaroo shit. The entire World Championship teams' delegations were accommodated in a beautiful tower block, Westaway Towers on Kings Beach, which after a few parties we nicknamed, appropriately, Wasteaway Towers. Typically, and as was always the case, we took with us to Australia some good old British weather so maximised on the warm, but overcast and windy first day, spending our time on a beautiful, golden beach where we indulged in surfing and swimming in the sea. It was to our peril spending so much time out on the surf however, as we didn't realise just how strong the Australian sun's rays are. We were all so terribly sunburned, the worst sufferers being ginger-haired Geoff and Tony, whose skin took on the tone of raw steak and them being so painfully sore, couldn't bear the agony of wearing a jumpsuits or let anyone take grips or even touch them when dirt-diving. After only one training jump, we decided it was too painful and had no choice but to stand down for a couple of days remaining in the shade (nicknamed the British Mushroom Team) while watching the rest of the world's teams training.

The World Championships took place at an Agricultural College in Gatton, Queensland, the accommodation available to all delegates from the nineteen nations competing. The accommodation and facilities were brilliant with just a short walk from the chalet-type rooms was a restaurant, swimming pool, bar, and oh, yes, I nearly forgot, a short grass strip for the jump aircraft to take off. The USA team, Mirror Image were in close contention for first place with the Germans, Canadians and French team and it was down to the last jump when USA secured gold on the last jump by one point. With perfect weather and just one aircraft flying from dawn to dusk, only stopping to refuel, the entire meet was completed in just three days which was an amazing feat for the organisers and judges.

Freddy Laker

Early Spring 1978, I packed my bags again and headed for Skydive Raeford, North Carolina, USA, for yet another training camp in Style and Accuracy. In the mid to late 70s, air travel to the USA was becoming popular and more and more airlines were offering cheaper flights, the best ever deal being Freddy Laker's no frills airline, Sky Train. The 'Fly me, I'm Freddy' deal offered a brand-new, revolutionary concept of economic air travel, requiring passengers to purchase their tickets on the day of travel and as meals were not part of the deal, passengers packed their own food for the journey. The cheap flights afforded me extra training funds which I spent on training jumps at Raeford, under the watchful eye of Gene-Paul Thacker.

I flew from London to New York paying only £59 for a one-way ticket on the airline's 345-seat McDonnell Douglas wide-bodied DC10 and continued the journey buying cheap internal 'stand-by' night flights to Charlotte and Fayetteville which is a short distance from Raeford. Internal flight in the States in those days was as easy as catching a bus in the UK and worked out much cheaper too. The late night standby flight from New York cost about $17 and after purchasing a ticket at the airline desk, I checked in my bags and boarded the aircraft, again without any form of ID or passport check.

Gene-Paul and Miss Billy were always most welcoming to us Brits when we arrived at their DZ and after a BBQ and few beers, I set up home, pitched my canvas tent in the woods and suspended a home-made hammock, made from an obsolete parachute, between two nearby pine trees. The hammock was sanctuary, a blissful place to lay after a long skydiving day when I'd open a can of dizzy stuff (Miller Lite) and look at the night skies through the tall, highly scented, pine tree canopy above me. Behind my tent ran the long tarmac runway, to the front a full view of the drop zone and pea-gravel pit. A short distance away in the woods, the skydiver driver's trailer was home to Dan Bossard. Dan became a great and long-standing friend who made 'full English' breakfasts whenever he had the opportunity, before strapping the Cessna to his ass and burn Avgas throughout the day flying us skydivers on one way journeys to altitude and throwing us out at the top. Dan was the ultimate skydiver driver!

Raeford DZ was home to a multitude of nationalities, each skydiver training in preparation for their own National Championships where most went on to take a place on National teams to compete at the forthcoming World Championships.

With so much talent on the drop zone, everyone's performance benefited and as the weeks went by, it was clear that any one of the skydivers training during that period could go on to be a world champion and, over the years, most did achieve world-champion status in their careers.

Gene-Paul had served on the United States Army Parachute Team, The Golden Knights, and in 1970, purchased the airport near Fort Bragg and opened the Raeford Parachute Centre. Over the years he coached, mentored and was a second father to a generation of skydivers making it the most popular drop zone in the world, not only for style and accuracy competitors but for relative workers too, and more World Champions emerged from his DZ than any other due to his all-round 'get things done' and bad-ass critiques. He said it like it was with no holds barred and regularly he'd comment after observing my performance with a humoured response, "What the hell you doin' girl? I'm wastin my time watching you?" The truth hurt but the only way to improve was to suck it up and take on board what he said.

Skydivers training at Raeford had the highest respect for Gene-Paul and always took on board his criticism making it work to their advantage. Yes, he was a hard task-master to please but he certainly got results. On the last lift of every day, he'd bet me $10 if I got a dead centre which was always an incentive, just to defy him. Skydiving is a far richer sport for having had Gene Paul Thacker on board and I for one, am so thankful for his kick-ass attitude which steered me to success.

After training for two whole months at Raeford, it was time to return to the UK to compete in the British National Championships. On Saturday 1st July 1978, the British skydiving contingency out there training, departed Raeford and with five days to travel, we thought we had ample time to recover from jet-lag in the UK before travelling the long road journey to Bridlington in Yorkshire. Competition registration was scheduled for the following Thursday, the competition commencing Friday 7th.

Our internal flight from Fayetteville/Charlotte touched down in New York and four of us Brits jumped into a yellow cab asking the driver to take us to Freddy Laker's ticket sales office, located on the gritty and then dangerously seedy Queens' Boulevard, Queens. The driver negotiated through traffic on New York's gridlocked roads honking his horn, while rudely gesticulating to other drivers. It was all in a normal day's work for him but we thought we were going to die when pedestrians jay-walked in front of us risking life and limb crossing streets while dodging speeding cars and trucks. Approaching Freddy Laker's ticket office lobby, the cab driver pointed to the long line (queue) of people stretching the length of the entire block, so we asked if he could drop us off at the end of the queue. He drove around the block and we discovered the end of the queue stretched around three sides of the block, the end of the queue nearly reaching the start of the queue. We jumped out of the taxi and joined those at the end, dropping our heavy parachuting equipment bags on the pavement.

Dane decided to investigate what was going on and returned some time later jokingly asking if we wanted the good news, or the bad news. There was no good news! The bad news was that from where we were in the queue, it would take three whole days and nights sleeping on Queens Boulevard before reaching the ticket lobby on perhaps the Tuesday or Wednesday before we could purchase our tickets home. The chances of us returning to the UK before the National Championships registration deadline the following Thursday looked slim and our chances of competing for a place on the British Team certainly looked in jeopardy.

Dane, Alan Leyton RIP, Bob Hiatt, and I formed a group with the others queuing alongside us, so we could look after each other's bags while sleeping or visiting local department stores to use the bathroom facilities, where bird-baths in the wash basins were the only option for personal hygiene. I dried my washed armpits over upturned hand dryers in New York's restrooms years before Madonna became famous for doing it.

In our group, a German army conscript was so desperate to fly back home, he telephoned all airlines at all locations across the United States searching for any connecting flight but due to it being national holidays, all flights were booked solid, therefore he and others trying the same, were unsuccessful. Another lady in our group was travelling to the UK to attend her grandmother's funeral, but she too was unsuccessful, leaving her in a state of devastation and disappointment.

Other than the $17 left in my wallet, I was totally out of money apart from my air fare home and National Championships entrance fee – there was no hole in the wall back then to withdraw money from bank accounts. Fortunately, on the opposite side of the road, was a lifesaving Baskin Robbins ice cream parlour, whose kind and generous staff dished out extra-large dollops of delicious strawberry shortcake double cone ice-creams for $1 to everyone queuing for flights. Ice-cream and water was all we lived on for three days and as much as I enjoyed ice-cream, I was pretty fed up with it after three days and yearned for a good meal, a nice cup of tea and most of all a shower. At night time, those queuing tucked into sleeping bags or makeshift beds and tents on the pavement (sidewalk) and those without sleeping bags, wore as many clothes as they could possibly get on.

During the night, local weirdos appeared and stood staring over us, one of which sat cross-legged on the pavement close to me preaching about Jesus. He looked not dissimilar to the convicted serial killer Charles Manson, who became an icon of evil in the 70s. His long greasy hair was in desperate need of an oil change, his straggly beard had morsels of food and nasal debris attached to it and his clothing stunk to high heaven of stale pee. The smell made me retch but I was too scared for my life to say anything to him, so avoided making eye contact and eventually he went away taking his smell with him. I breathed a sigh of relief and finally closed my eyes but the hustle and bustle of noisy traffic kept sleep at bay.

At about 3am, screeching brakes awakened those lucky enough to have fallen asleep and a car skidded to a halt, close by to where we lay. The car door opened, a body was flung onto the road then the vehicle's wheels screeched again as it disappeared into the night. Other drivers travelling at speed in the night-time traffic obviously didn't see the man's body lying in the road and drove their vehicles over it. It really was the most gruesome sight I have ever witnessed! Within seconds, police car sirens and flashing lights surrounded the body, the scene emerging before us looked like an episode of Starsky and Hutch but it wasn't a film in the making, it was for real.

Eventually, after the third night on the streets, we reached the airline desk and purchased our one-way ticket back to the UK. Our flight was scheduled for Tuesday 5th June, giving us just two days to get home and drive the long journey north to Bridlington. Every passenger on that aircraft had spent the previous three nights on the streets and in a collective cheer, celebrated together once on board and seated. After such an ordeal, it was a huge relief to be on our way home at last.

British Team Selection – National Championships – Bridlington

After paying my entry fees to compete in Individual Accuracy, Team Accuracy and Individual Style my next, and most important port of call, was to find a quiet corner in a field full of cow pats to pitch my tent in the darkness. At last, I had time to relax before the competition commenced and the following days proved most important with no margin for error in qualifying for selection on my fourth British Team, three previously in Style and Accuracy in 1974 Szolnok Hungary, 1976 Guidonia, Italy and the third in 1977 in Gatton, Australia as a member of the British 8-Way Team, Symbiosis. Competitors' names were placed in a hat and the order of jump 'draw' took place defining the order in which each person jumped throughout the ten-jump competition. Blow me! I was drawn first as Number 1 meaning a very early o'clock start on the first lift, wheels off at 4.30am the following day.

Exhausted from travelling from America, jet lag on top of the long drive from Farnborough to Bridlington, I prayed for a beer front (bad weather) to descend upon the drop zone so I could have a sleep in but that wasn't to be. Before any accuracy competition commences each day, competitors trudge to the pit to watch the WIDI load when a group of non-competitors throw a wind drift indicator from the aircraft directly over the landing area for the accuracy event, to get a feel for the wind direction, observing any deviations or dog-legs, and also strength. After flight-line checks, I approached the rear of the Cessna aircraft, its spinning propeller blowing away the sleep from my eyes as I leaned into the blasting air. The bonus of being on the first lift of the day are the amazing visuals from the open door, the crystal clear skies and gorgeous arrays of colour from cerulean blue on the horizon to darkest indigo high above. Looking out the aircraft door, I watched the large glowing sphere of the sun cast sunbeams far and wide distracting me from my 'in-competition' zone and wished I could remain there longer to relish the bird's eye view of dawn. The aircraft levelled out and the pilot's words, 'running in' snapped me quickly into the zone again and it was time to bring it on.

Each competitor decides their own exit point to jump and as expert as the pilots are at flying the aircraft, they sometimes require some degree of correction in their aircraft headings and the skydiver looking out the aircraft door may give 'five (degrees) left' or 'five (degrees) right' to fly directly over their desired exit point. The tiny electronically measured target is each competitor's ultimate aim on each competition jump and whoever scores the least amount of distance totalled for the competition jumps is the most accurate in the competition, winning gold. Most competitors can fly their parachute to the electronic target 'pad' which is a skill in its own right but it is all down to the final inch where foot placement requires great 'hand-and-eye-to-foot' co-ordination to place the heel precisely on the button. It is a matter of who is the best on the day.

Bridlington was by far one of the trickiest places I ever competed, where the upper and lower winds varied by 180 degrees in direction and where temperature inversions occurred on a regular basis meaning the air at altitude was warmer than at a lower altitude. Also, there was occasionally a high consequence, immediately after take-off, of losing visibility of the airfield altogether when sea-fret, a wet mist or haze, spread inland from the sea, rapidly covering the airfield, at which time the pilot had no other option but to land the aircraft at another location. On one occasion, I exited the aircraft at 2,500ft with a clear view of the drop zone below me and not a cloud in the sky. Within seconds of my parachute opening, I watched helplessly as the sea-fret and mist approached like a tsunami wave obscuring the airfield below. Flying my parachute 'blind' into the sea-fret was a very watery experience like flying through a heavy rain shower and on a few occasions at Bridlington, I touched down looking like I'd dived into a swimming pool with all my gear on. As adverse as Bridlington's climate was, it was an ideal training DZ to experience parachute flight in severe wind shears and 180-degree dog-legs where I learned to make judgemental approaches to achieve good results by hitting the target. Flying a parachute expertly with finely honed skills is one thing, assessing the winds on each and every jump of every competition is another skill only achieved by lots of practice and experience. There is no short-cut to success.

The training camp at Raeford paid off however and with relief I became National Champion again, with gold in all ladies' events and being selected as a British Team member again for the fourth time to represent Great Britain on the world's stage filled me with pride. For those of us who'd successfully made it onto the British Team, it was just a stepping stone to something much bigger. On this occasion I personally felt I'd peaked at the right time and was a strong contender for a medal in the World Championships medal race.

British Team Training

It hadn't seemed like two minutes since I was sleeping on the streets of Queens Boulevard, New York, attempting to return to the UK but those making British Team selection were soon to be airborne crossing the Atlantic en-route to Raeford, North Carolina again. My personal funds were totally spent on training; entry fees for the National Champs, travel and food, and at the Visa Immigration desk on arrival in USA, the clerk who checked my passport asked how long I intended staying in the USA. I replied, "two weeks". He then asked how much money I carried on me for the duration of my stay. When I told him "about $20" the passport clerk called security who, while not inflicting pain, physical or mental torture to extract information from me, whizzed me into a room to question my intentions in USA. Bob King, British Team Coach, quickly came to my rescue vouching that my living, travel and incidental costs would be taken care of out of the allocated British Parachute Association Team fund, on which he pulled the purse strings. Hilariously, Bob then had to sign as my guarantor, accepting full responsibility for me and my expenses while I was in the USA.

The following two weeks became a matter of routine as I'd already spent six weeks at Raeford DZ prior to the National Championships. The tent pitched in the exact spot as previously, the tent pegs hammered into the exact same holes and the parachute material hammock remained hanging between the two trees swinging gently in the breeze, tempting me to adorn it again. It was home-from-home and I quickly settled into my life-on-the-drop zone routine where the fresh outdoor scent of damp, pine-filled air filled up my senses again. Day in, day out, the Brit team completed eight or more jumps, four or five in the morning and then four more in the late afternoon with a 'too hot to jump' weather break midday. The temperatures were far hotter than during my previous training trip and thermal monsters swirled around the drop zone spinning this way and that way, collecting dust particles and small stones into their vertical flow. Encountering a dust devil or 'eddy' while flying a parachute towards the target became a whole new game of survival, when the parachute flew unpredictably, bouncing up and up, down and down and causing such hard landings that we were lucky to walk away from them. I still sting from some of those arrivals on the ground. When the weather conditions became too hazardous to parachute, the hardest decision to make was either take a dip in the cool lake across from the airfield or take refuge from the glaring sun and spend the afternoon swaying in the hammock in the shade of the pine trees.

Decisions, decisions! Away from the usual trappings of nine-to-five work it wasn't such a hard choice to make.

On my final training jump before travelling to the World Championships, my trusty old Strato-Star canopy, a five-cell ram air square parachute, had broken some lines, resulting in a rotating malfunction and me cutting it away to deploy my reserve parachute. The canopy had over 1,000 jumps on it and was showing signs of wear and tear especially after the previous two years jumping and competing in World Championships in Italy and in the Australian sunshine. The lines were old and frayed and desperately needed replacing so that very night, while the remainder of the British Team went out for a meal and beer, a very special friend, Mark Limond, a US Parachute Team member and parachute rigger, worked with me into the night replacing the complete line-set. Mark did most of the work, measuring up the old lines and attaching the new ones to the exact same length and trim accounting for line-stretch when the canopy opened the first few times. Mark, if you are reading this, I am totally indebted to you and your expertise that evening and I have no doubt that without your assistance, I am certain I might not have achieved what I did at that World Championships. From the bottom of my heart, 'THANK YOU' from a most appreciative World Champion Brit. Cheers mate!

On Top of The World – World Champion

World Championships – Zagreb 1978

Training completed, the next port of call was home to Blighty for a few days to refresh and recharge before travelling to the World Championships in Zagreb, (formerly) Yugoslavia. Qualifying national teams were accommodated in a high-rise building in the centre of Zagreb and coaches ferried competitors, judges and officials to and from the airfield each day. The 14th World Championships opening ceremony took place on the drop zone watched by dignitaries and locals, after which, we competitors were allowed one practice jump to acclimatise to weather conditions and get a feel for the AN2 (Antonov) aircraft and get aerial bearings. Every competitor, the best in the world from each country, surrounded the landing area 'pit' to observe the practice jumps assessing not only the weather conditions but also other competitor's form. On my newly-lined canopy, I scored 0.00cm on the practice jump and received a round of applause as I walked from the pit towards the British Team tent. My canopy, my trusty blue and white Strato-Star, was out-dated and 'so last year' in parachuting trends. Most competitors were using larger parachutes enabling a much slower descent, which allowed more time for foot placement on the small target. Some scoffed at my canopy and asked why I was still jumping the near-to-its-end-of-life parachute advising me to get a better one to give me any chance of a medal in the competition. The negative banter didn't affect me one iota and as I walked towards the Brit team tent, I observed the Union Jack blowing in the breeze. I felt so proud and an overwhelming feeling of confidence swept over me when I said to myself, "Yep! This one's mine! I'm going to win this!"

Throughout the first day of competition, I completed three accuracy jumps scoring 0.00cm on the electronic 'button' on each. At the end of the day, the coaches returned the competitors to the accommodation in Zagreb and later that evening I was filled with a strong positive feeling, not in an arrogant or cocky way, but I just felt I was going to win. With three perfect jumps in the bag, I was all too aware that seven more jumps remained before the competition was complete and for every jump I classed it as a one jump shoot-out aware that the only person I was competing against was me, myself and I. To win the competition I had to achieve 0.00cm on every jump and anything less meant I'd lose the competition. The following morning the Individual Style event commenced (where competitors perform aerobatic manoeuvres, turns and back loops in timed events). After performing two style jumps, I heard my name being called giving me twenty minutes notice prior to boarding the aircraft to complete my fourth round of accuracy. In the middle of the day when the heat bouncing off the pea-gravel became visible like wavy air rising in a mirage, the windsock hung lifeless for periods of time, before filling and standing out straight as if a gale was blowing through. Thermals did some weird things to the windsock that day. One second it was filled with air and pointing skywards making it look as though the wind was blowing upwards whereas in fact it was the thermal activity lifting it up. The windsock deflated and hung limp again, then swung through 180 degrees in the opposite directions before emptying and falling lifeless again. Every accuracy competitor hoped the winds remained a constant speed blowing straight and in one direction but in the scorching heat of the day, experienced competitors accepted that wasn't going to happen. Controlling the canopy on final approach towards the target in such unpredictable conditions is hard work and I knew I was going to have my wits about me to land in the pit, let alone score 0.00cm. Working the canopy's brakes to ensure it kept its forward movement while remaining on the attack 'wire' directly on the wind-line towards the electronic pad, was similar to riding a bucking bronco in the thermals. As I approached the edge of the hot pea gravel, the thermal activity lifted my canopy ballooning upwards and in a split second, I sat 20ft higher than I was comfortable with. Resisting the urge to stop the canopy flying forward, the canopy swiftly descended again and I regained control as I flew through the turbulent air. The dropping sensation after flying through a thermal is similar to being in an elevator and under the canopy there isn't much to do about it. Hovering above the pad, I placed my foot accurately in the centre and struck with my heal scoring a fourth 0.00cm. It certainly wasn't the easiest of approaches to the target I'd ever made and I didn't get any Brownie points for neatness but I controlled the parachute and at the end of the day, it is the score that counts.

At that stage in the competition with four 0.00cm back-to-back jumps, there was a buzz around in the drop-zone and other competitors began to watch my every jump. Some competitors told me that 'so-and-so' was doing well and chasing my tail, but I stuck my fingers in my ears and mumbled, "La la la la la" to blank out what they were saying. The only score I was interested in was my own. From then on I took long, sweeping detours around the drop zone to avoid glancing upon large white score-boards screens. Earlier that day however, I'd witnessed my friend, rival and previous world champion, Cheryl Stearns, who scored 0.02cm on the electronic read-out. I didn't let that suck me into competing with her score. Two centimetres is a big lead in competition, but I certainly couldn't cut any slack and relax. Day four dawned and favourable weather conditions prevailed throughout the day, allowing all 260 competitors to complete five further accuracy jumps. On each and every descent I approached the target from a different angle and direction, this way and that way depending on the fickle wind or thermal activity, striking with either left or right heel. On each jump, for the split second I sat in the pea-gravel after each landing, the anticipation from not only myself and others watching increased while awaiting the electronic monitor to register the score. Every time I landed, 0.00cm lit up and loud cheering from the British Team members filled the air. It was amazing and each time a huge relief for me. After nine 0.00cm scores, my stomach churned like a washing machine and I was beginning to feel nervous and nauseous. I acknowledged in my head that it was a one-jump competition on the 10th and final jump. There were two scenarios facing me; one of ecstatic pleasure or one of heartache and disappointment; the joy of success achieving World Champion status, or the disappointment of being an also-ran. If I messed up on that tenth jump, I would at least have been remembered for keeping the rest of the competition on their toes for the other nine rounds.

The pressure suddenly hit me and I needed to be alone in a solitary place to remain in my own little zone. I couldn't just sit around as usual and chit-chat and I couldn't focus on anyone else's words. Out of politeness I excused myself, withdrawing somewhere out of view where I could find quiet solace and where I could stew in my own space. For the following two and a half days, the weather conditions remained unfavourable and competitors were put on constant 'bad weather holds' with winds 'over the limits' and the low thundery clouds and torrential rain kept us well and truly grounded. Drop zones are miserable places to be when parachuting is stopped due to inclement weather but during those two and a half days, I was sitting on nine x 0.00cms with the World Championships title hanging like a fragile thread from my shoulders. No pressure then! Other competitors gave me encouraging pats on the back offering support commenting, "Hope you are the first person in the world to get 10 x 0.00cm" and as much as I truly appreciated everyone's kind words of encouragement I really, really, really did not want to hear them at that time. My place of solace and retreat was behind the British Team tent where I could be in my own space, in my own zone. Everyone handles pressure differently and I always found apprehension provided me with the right amount of adrenalin to maximise my concentration for my best performance, but I have to be in a very quiet and personal zone to nurture it.

John Meacock, the Brit Team Head of Delegation, was incredibly supportive totally appreciating the pressure I was under and knew exactly where I was at in my head. He spent most of his time protecting my space and guarding my quiet 'zone' deterring anyone from joining me and John, if you are reading this, I am eternally grateful to you for your support. After two nights of sleep deprivation, tossing and turning, snoozing for brief moments, then wakening in a shocked panic state, I imagined (and believed) someone was in the room and looking over me. I could have been struck off rations and handed in my bedding for all the use my bed and food were to me during those few days. On the third day, we boarded the coaches outside the accommodation in Zagreb and again drove out to the drop zone where the weather conditions hadn't changed but the forecast was more favourable later in the day. Competitors at this stage were entertaining themselves by either kicking a ball about, playing hacky (a DZ game of keepy-uppy with a small leather sac), volley ball, cricket, performing handstands and gymnastics, riding mono-cycles or just lying around like skydivers do when they are bored. The drop zone looked more like a circus training camp than a World Parachuting Championships. Again I retreated to the rear of the Brit Team Tent when an announcement echoed over the PA system calling all accuracy judges to the pit, the landing area. The accuracy event was about to commence in thirty minutes' time so I checked and re-checked my parachuting equipment and walked out to the 'pit' to watch the wind drift indicator to observe the weather conditions. I made my own personal analysis of where to get out of the aircraft and given the wind direction and strength, my approximate set-up point where I might approach the target from. I heard my name being called giving me thirty minutes to kit up and prepare for the acid test, my 10th accuracy jump at the 14th World Championships. It was 1st September 1978 and I heard, "Jacqueline Smith; Great Britain; Helmet number 244; this is your thirty-minute call". This was it. But hold on, bladder goes into overdrive and declares "Nervous pee time!" I went for five nervous pees and each time I sat down it was a waste of time, nothing happened apart from me warming the toilet seat. I made my way to the pit area and watched the three aircraft lifts prior to mine, observing the other competitors' final approaches and how their parachutes were flying in the surface winds.

Again, the windsock was playing silly buggers, filling up with hot air from thermal activity, falling limp, and seconds later filling up and changing direction by 180 degrees. John Meacock assisted me in kitting up by lifting my parachuting harness off the ground and placing it on my shoulders. The parachuting equipment wasn't heavy, but the enormous weight on my shoulders at this time certainly was. John was ten times more nervous than me and you'd have thought it was him kitting up for the tenth round and standing close to me, face to face, he made 'knowing' eye contact but didn't speak. No words were necessary, I read the message in his eyes loud and clear, his silent 'good luck' nod was deafeningly clear. John had been an inspiration to me for a long, long time, being the leading figure in British sport parachuting, being National Champion on numerous occasions, and he was the successful owner of Peterborough Parachute Centre. John didn't suffer fools kindly and if his expectations of those who trained under his critical eye did not reach his high expectations, then he certainly didn't hold back dishing out colourful expletives and criticism. He strived for perfection and did not tolerate or have the time of day for anyone who didn't do similarly and give it 100% effort. At that 14th World Championships, it was the first time John was not competing himself but instead was Head of Delegation. He wanted the success of a British gold medal more than anything and I'm so glad he was there to witness me achieve it.

Fully kitted up and ready to walk out to the aircraft with the other competitors on the same lift, John shadowed my every step carefully, shielding me from the multitude of TV crews, reporters and other competitors. The air was electric with excitement. No-one in the world had ever achieved ten consecutive back-to-back jumps scoring 0.00cm on an electronic target before, not anyone, male or female and it was something everyone on the drop zone wanted to witness, but no-one wanted it more than me. I climbed the steps into the Antonov AN2 door-frame taking one long glance back towards the windsock at the target area, noting the wind conditions one final time, then walked into the aircraft and I sat down. I was to be fifth out of the aircraft, so positioned myself where I was able to see the other jumpers exit individually and in sequence before me. In doing so, I could view from the open door the ever-changing weather and surface winds below and observe where the other canopies were landing. The pilot flew the aircraft in huge circuits over and around the drop zone and on each circuit, one competitor launched from the door, deploying their parachute within a few seconds after hitting the slipstream. I watched the first jumper exit the aircraft and as she fell away, gave me the thumbs up before deploying her parachute. The aircraft continued into another circuit over the airfield and the next competitor wished me luck before leaping out over the exact same spot. As the fourth competitor exited the aircraft, I looked to the ground and saw the second girl to jump landing outside the target area to the left of the pit. At that point, the co-pilot brushed past me walking quickly to the rear of the aircraft where he closed the door. He looked me in the eye, circled his finger in the air and from both closed fists proceeded to open and close, stretching his fingers, indicating, ten; twenty (minutes); shrugged his shoulders and made an upside down smile indicating he couldn't communicate in English. For some reason unbeknown to me, the aircraft had to hold off and circle above the DZ for twenty minutes or so until the ground-to-air signal gave us the clear to drop again. There wasn't really a language barrier as I understood exactly what his animated hand gestures meant. Skydivers usually communicate with eye/hand 'speak' but the only thing the co-pilot couldn't communicate to me was the reason for being held off. Looking out the aircraft window to where the previous jumpers had landed, their canopies visible on the ground below, one lying to one side of the pit, the others were lying on the grass at a distance short of the target area. I didn't know what to make of the situation but guessed that the winds had perhaps increased in strength or maybe had changed direction but I couldn't be sure so had to remain calm. I loosened my harness leg straps, leaned against my backpack, took off my leather frappe hat helmet and closed my eyes attempting to block out any silly mind games; meanwhile the pilot flew around and around the drop zone time and time again, maintaining the jump altitude of 2,500ft with each circuit. After an agonising thirty-five minutes or so, the co-pilot brushed past me again, tapped my shoulder before re-opening the aircraft's rear exit door. He pointed to his eye, then to me and finally to the door indicating I was to be the next one to jump on the next circuit over the drop zone. On jump run, I gave two ten degrees' corrections to the left to get me on line to where I wanted to exit and as loud as the aircraft engines growled, they were drowned out by my heartbeat pounding in my ears. Prior to exiting I looked down at the exit and took one long deep breath, exhaled slowly then stepped out into the slipstream. Looking up to watch the aircraft continue flying away, I energetically threw out my pilot chute and watched the parachute bag lift off my back. The stowed lines released in slow motion until they reached full line stretch and the parachute inflated, decelerating my fall rate. Perhaps it was the adrenalin surging through my veins that made everything in slow motion, but my canopy appeared to stream for a couple of seconds before I took hold of the risers to give them a good shake. Having a malfunction and cutting away was the last thing I needed right then and eventually my canopy opened with a bang, sending the slider whizzing down the lines.

I took the steering toggles out of their keepers and glanced down immediately to locate the target and windsock, to assess the wind strength and direction. I then looked up and spoke to my canopy saying, "Just one more time; just one more dead-centre!" Because I'd been airborne and circling over the airfield in the AN2 aircraft for such a long period of time, I'd no idea what the wind conditions were like on the ground, so it was important for me to play it safe. My plan was to stay close to the target as the air was very hot and humid and I knew I could easily slow my parachute's forward flight in the heavy, moist air. If I set up on final approach too far away from the target area, the winds might be too strong to allow my parachute to penetrate forward and if there was anything I didn't want to do was drop short. It was the hottest period of the day and in the searing heat, monstrous thermal activity resulted in some weird windsock activity blowing this way, then that way, this way and that way again; it hung limp then inflated as if a gale was blasting through it. At one stage the windsock actually pointed upwards towards me and from my height of 1,500ft looking down, it was impossible to hazard a guess which was the true wind line. To make an approach to the target, I needed to be on the wind line (or as close to it as I possibly could be considering the conditions) to ensure I could fly 'down the wire', into wind as I approached the target. I set up on my attack point to approach the target and realised I was far too hot; uncomfortably close to the target and way too high. I flew an incredibly steep angle (I called it the angle of the dangle) and it looked good, a tad closer than I'd have really liked to be but I was in control and feeling comfortable. As I flew slowly over the edge of the pit, my canopy ballooned upwards, picked up by a thermal, so I eased off the brakes slightly to increase the canopy's forward drive and to fly through it, then immediately applied deep brakes again to reduce my forward speed. Descending to about 10 feet above the target with both hands gently tweaking the canopy's flight path with my eyes firmly focussed on the dead-centre, I became aware of my right foot twitching. I'm usually perfectly still under the canopy on final approach as any body movement, apart from the hands and arms, can affect the canopy's flight and twitching was something I'd never experienced before. I made a split-second decision to use my left foot, and struck with my heel, placing it positively on the dead centre. My bum hit the pea-gravel a second later and although I knew I'd planted the disc good and proper, I glanced across to the electronic read-out and waited for what seemed a lifetime before 0.00 lit up on the screen. I closed my eyes, took a humongous sigh of relief, then laid back into my open parachute container and harness nestling my head in the pea-gravel.

The whole drop zone went berserk, the judges were jumping up and down cheering me and the rest of the world's competitor's danced jigs, whooped, hollered, clapped and cheered. My fellow British team mates ran into the pit to where I was sitting, then picked me up and carried me and my canopy towards the British Team tent accompanied by an ecstatic and overjoyed Doug Peacock, the accuracy event judge, who abandoned his position in the pit to congratulate me. If I had a pound for every pat on my back and congratulatory kiss, then I'd surely be a millionaire. It was magical; I laughed uncontrollably while crying tears of joy and at the same time, smiling like a Cheshire cat. I could hear myself speaking out loud "I did it! Me? Me? Me? Me? I did it! No! It can't be me! I must be dreaming! Me? Me? Surely not! Me? Me? Me? No! It can't be true! No! No! Not me! Surely not! Me? Me?" I saw Dane's unshaven face; his smile spread wide across his face from ear to ear... he was just the proudest person on the planet and so pleased for me. From the day I scored the five 0.00cm scores, Dane became uncharacteristically superstitious, sticking religiously to the same daily routine right down to not shaving and hearsay had it he wore the same clothing and (washed) underpants every day. Our Head of Delegation, John Meacock, presented a bouquet of beautiful red roses, ten of them, being one for each of the dead-centres I'd scored and such was the moment, John put his hands over his eyes to wipe away tears of joy exposing a side to John Meacock I was privileged to witness. Euphoria in such magnitude is something I wish I could bottle to share with everyone to savour and experience the amazing feeling.

Later, when my breathing and heart rate had returned to normal, John Meacock told me the reason the aircraft had been put on hold for so long resulting in the thirty-five-minute delay before I was allowed to jump, was because the Turkish competitor who had jumped prior to me, had taken a really hard landing in the pit (landing area) and required medical assistance. She had to remain still and couldn't be moved as the medics suspected she had a spinal injury and only when she was stretchered away was the pilot given the instruction 'clear to drop'. John Meacock had, while the aircraft circled overhead, written a letter of protest requesting a re-jump had I messed up on my tenth jump but after I landed successfully and scored 0.00cm, he took great pleasure in tearing it up as he had no reason to submit it. I was the absolute WORLD CHAMPION, a first for Great Britain and a first for the world in both male and female competition!

At the end of the day the coaches collected the competitors, returning us to the hotel in the centre of Zagreb and for some reason, I was detained in my seat while everyone else queued in the aisle before leaving the bus ahead of me. Inside the hotel long queues of competitors waited for the lifts, so I opted to climb the stairs to the 10th floor. The rooms didn't have en-suite bathrooms and each floor had two climb-in, sit-up-type baths which had to cater for thirty or so competitors. It appeared that I was the last in the queue and had to wait for ages for a shower but with victory racing through my veins, I was as happy as Larry, on cloud nine and buzzing like World Champions do.

Eventually, a bathroom became free and I climbed into the chair-like bath and typically, there was no hot water left, so showered in the cold, murky-brown water, and hurriedly dried my hair and dressed for dinner. Aware I might be late for the meal, I descended the stairs jumping four steps at a time and as I pushed open the swing doors leading into the main eating hall, I was welcomed by loud cheers and applause which nearly blew me off my feet. Everyone involved in the championships, competitors, judges, dignitaries and hosts gave a standing ovation for an overly long time when flowers, gifts and congratulations came at me from all directions. Oh how sweet those moments on the world's stage, I am one very lucky girl indeed.

Leading up to my tenth jump I hadn't eaten much so once the pressure was off the pangs of hunger hit me, I was starving and could have eaten a horse. The waiter service in the hotel that night was particularly slow so in celebration, I threw glass after glass of cold, bubbling champagne down my neck perhaps giving the impression I was drinking for Great Britain. As one glass emptied, another appeared in my hand and given the atmosphere and circumstance and not wanting to be rude, I had to oblige and drink everything that was put in front of me. The room began to spin and as it went round for the third or fourth time, I put my hand out to steady it gibbering, like drunkards do, about being under the affluence of incahol, being a little slort of sheep, not knowing who is me yet and the drunker I stood there, the longer I got insisting I was not as drunk as thinkle peep I was.

Apparently the rest of the Brit team carried me up to my room and threw me on the bed before returning to the bar to celebrate my gold medal, meanwhile, I zonked out for the night oblivious of the good time I was missing. You know that feeling when you wake up after a heavy drinking session and you can't remember what had happened? Well apart from a thumping headache and hangover, I wasn't really sure if I'd dreamt the whole thing and still had the tenth jump to complete.

On the drop zone later that day, the organisers were in a bit of a quandary due to not having a Union Flag for the medal ceremony and neither did they have a copy of the British National Anthem. I heard my name booming over the PA system, "Jacqueline Smith of Great Britain, World Champion" and I stepped up the two stairs onto the middle of the podium. I was as nervous as I'd been on my tenth jump and as I bent forward to shake hands and receive my medal, was given a strong, tight and lengthy handshake by the head of Federation Aviation International (FAI) who I thought was never going to let go. The audience of world class skydivers from every nation along with judges, organisers and spectators roared a big cheer and then the air filled with whistling, whooping and celebratory applause. What an incredible feeling! I turned right to watch the Union Flag being slowly hoisted, below it the second and third place flags of United States of America and Russia then the first five words of the National Anthem boomed out, "God Save Our Gracious Queen". Overwhelmed by the occasion I went deaf, didn't hear the rest of the National Anthem and I became uncontrollably emotional, sobbing and crying. It really was the most incredibly proud moment in my life and even now, years later, when I hear the National Anthem, it brings a tear to my eye.

Returning to the UK was something of a shock to my system. I was penniless, as poor as a church mouse with no money to pay my rent. Great Britain was in the grips of the Iron Lady's (Maggie Thatcher) winter of discontent when she introduced legislation to curb trade unions' power, whose leadership she accused of undermining parliamentary democracy and economic performance through strike action. In response to Maggie's legislation, several local authority trade unions nationwide launched further strikes demanding larger pay rises. The whole country was in turmoil when the public sector took strike actions when even the grave-diggers in Liverpool refused to work and refuse was left to the rats on the streets of Britain. I attended three job interviews on one day but was unsuccessful and resorted to selling everything I owned, including my trusty Strato-Star and the rest of my parachuting equipment. The BPA was in turmoil when I returned from the World Championships and the Secretary General was asked to resign, which he did, and my record-breaking achievement and World Champion status were overlooked entirely, like it never happened. In fact, it took 19 years for the then BPA Chairman, Phil Gibbs, to formally congratulate me on my achievement of being World Champion and awarded 'Life' membership to me. I was also nominated in the late 90s for my achievements to the Royal Aero Club of Great Britain and was awarded the Gold medal joining the ranks of Bleriot, The Wright brothers, de Havilland and other aviators for outstanding achievement. At the end of 1978 the BBC invited me to attend the Sports Personality of the Year show and David Coleman, the presenter, gave me a congratulatory mention, and I sat in the second row, behind all the TV sports personalities, Ian Botham, Steve Ovett, Daley Thompson and Ray Reardon. The rest of the audience was made up of World Champions, just like myself, all resigned to the knowledge 'we' wouldn't win. It was a foregone conclusion that the winning personality was going to be a high profile personality from a sport which had maximum media coverage. I met other female World Champions at the BBC TV Studio and one of them asked for my address as she wanted to nominate me to attend the Women of the Year Luncheon in the Savoy, London which I cordially accepted. What an honour it was to attend the luncheon where I met inspiring women from all walks of life, listened to speeches and shared a table with Molly Sugden (from Are You Being Served) and the yachtswoman Naomi James. If 1978 couldn't get any better, I was then entered into the Guinness Book of World Records for being the first person, male or female, to score ten perfect scores on an electronic measuring pad at a World Parachuting Championships.

1979

1979 proved to be equally as exciting, starting with a nice little jolly to Dubai by special invitation of ex-SAS Pete Sherman who led and coached from its infancy, the United Arab Emirates team in style and accuracy. Pete had organised a Classics competition for the Arabs and myself, Dougie Peacock, Dave Waugh, Jim Walmsley and a few others were to assist in judging but the competition was cancelled. There was nothing else to do for the following two weeks but kick back and enjoy the wall-to-wall blue skies, sun, sand, and sea. We skydived in the mornings until it became too hot, jumping out of Hueys and Aeritalia G222 (similar to a small C130) where Pete (at long last) docked 8th achieving his Star Crest Solo (SCS badge). When we weren't skydiving, we were sailing the balmy sea waters in Billy Foulkes' catamaran or swimming/socialising in the traditional British Red Lion pub, the first of its kind and like no other establishment at the time in Dubai. Like I said earlier, a tough life, but someone had to live it!

Symbiosis clinched a fabulous sponsorship deal with KP who asked us to do a TV commercial advertising a new product, KP Skydiver crisps. The sponsorship came with a tidy financial package, enough to pay for most of our training jumps, the bonus being a brand new set of colour co-ordinated equipment for each of us. It doesn't get much better than that and for two weeks KPs advertising agency travelled with us to Pope Valley, California where they filmed the ground and close-up shots. Meanwhile, Rande DeLuca, of the USA world champion team Mirror Image was on location, filming the in-air fighting scenes for the James Bond movie, Moonraker with BJ Worth and Jake Lombard and also filmed our in-air antics for the KP advertisement. When the filming was in the can, the advertising agents left for the UK to process the films, meanwhile we spent a further four weeks on the DZ, 4-way and 8-way training and having enough time and money to take time out from serious team training and indulge in high quality and fun big-way formation skydives with the other amazing and talented skydivers on the drop zone.

The 1979 National Championships was hosted at Netheravon where, for the first time, every discipline took place during the entire week which meant there was no opportunity for me to compete, as I would have liked to, in style and accuracy as well as 4 and 8-way. Symbiosis won gold and silver in the 4-way (two teams) and also won the 8-way with other 'Symbions' taking silver with their team, Formeight. Our 1st place team couldn't represent Great Britain at the upcoming World Championships however because we had three foreign nationals on the team, with Scooter USA, Bluebaker Australia, and Dave Wagner from Canada, leaving Rob, Geoff, William, Geoff and me. The British 8-way team evolved from other medallists including Robin Mills, Tim Andrewes, Stevie Newton, Tony Uragallo, Mike Smith, Fred and Jim Keery and myself with Bob Hiatt and Tim Kirkstead-Moore as alternates.

Immediately after the National Championships, five of us Symbiosis members flew out to Pope Valley again for another two-week training camp in 4-way, then travelled to Tecumseh, Michigan, to join up with the rest of the British contingent. The aircraft selected for the World Championships was a Nord Atlas, so the USA and Canadian teams pooled together to share the cost of a Skyvan in order to train and familiarise with the tailgate launch. Our host with the most (he really did push out the boat to greet us), Harold Lange, together with the local town folk, arranged a welcoming reception for all three teams and also opened their doors offering accommodation in their homes to individuals and small groups for the duration of the training camp. Us Brits very much appreciated the home-from-home experience, relaxing in a bed every evening after a day on the drop zone, a far cry from sleeping in a sleeping bag in a tent on the DZ. Tecumseh is located between three of the Great Lakes, Michigan, Huron and Erie and has some of the most severe weather conditions us Brits had ever seen. On one particular jump, all four seasons arrived in one day, the highlight being when an ominous-looking cloud arrived over the DZ at exactly the same time all three teams were under the canopy. The storm fostered heavy rain and damaging hail accompanied by strong updrafts of air resulting in some team members rising thousands of feet and contemplating what to do if they reached thinner and less oxygenated air. Some contemplated cutting away their main canopies, freefalling down to lower altitude and deploying their reserve parachutes but fortunately no-one had to resort to such measures. The winds were blowing a hooley, swirling in all directions, not one of us landed anywhere near the DZ and in fact we were so spread out around the town, the local fire brigade were called out to assist if anyone landed in trees or power lines. Amazingly, everyone survived to tell the tale with no injuries or equipment damage. Within thirty minutes, the calm after the storm appeared, and the sky was blue again with warm, light winds.

When the weather wasn't good for skydiving, the norm was to seek out other things to do and we made our way to a lake close by and tried our hands at water-skiing. For me, it was the first time I'd tried the sport and dressed only in a skimpy bikini, launched from the jetty into the deep water and after a few wobbles stood up like a pro (well, I'd like to think I did) and enjoyed the speed being towed around the lake. "Pfffft, this is easy" I thought and decided to be a bit more adventurous, criss-crossing behind the boat's wake when the inevitable happened and I performed the most spectacular wipe-out, flick-flacking across the lake's surface. The boat circled around, pulled up alongside me and the lads hoisted me on-board where they laughed uncontrollably while pointing to my nether regions. When I looked down to see what they were laughing at, to my horror, saw my bottom half completely exposed. The bikini I was wearing cost $10 at a local store in Tecumseh and in one swift rush of gushing water $9.50's worth of it had disappeared up my bum. I gingerly removed my bikini bottom from its temporary lodgings and fortunately suffered no internal injury from my rectal douche and from then on, I stuck to skydiving... far less dangerous a sport than water skiing!

The word on the street was out that the Brits were in town and Jim West, DZ owner of Greene County drop zone at Xenia, Ohio, invited us over to do some training jumps on his drop zone and as a thank you, we arranged a fun 10-way with him and Patty Valley docking 9th and tenth. As a thank you he threw a massive BBQ party for not only the skydivers but everyone in Xenia and the locals came up to meet us, we were treated like royalty. It never ceases to amaze me how kind and hospitable the skydiving community are and on the occasion we visited Xenia, the locals pulled out all the stops welcoming us with heart-warming hospitality.

Training over, both the Symbiosis 4-way team and 8-way team travelled by road from the UK to Chateauroux, France where we were taken to our Spartan military barracks accommodation about three miles from the DZ. The organisers separated me from my team, accommodating them in a separate block from mine which was some distance away. Tired and dirty from the journey, I made my way to the showers where I heard men's voices and discovered a load of bollock naked French soldiers who took great delight in waving their penises at me, while beckoning me to join them in the showers. I made a hasty retreat to my room, gathered my bags and ran in the direction of the British Team men's block and found our Head of Delegation discussing his dissatisfaction with the accommodation, especially as the French Team were languishing in 3-Star hotel directly across the road from the drop zone. En masse, we returned to the drop zone and he demanded we be relocated in better digs, together, and we too were given rooms in the same hotel as the French Team. The World Championships was a great success and we Brits took a silver in the 4-way and came in a creditable 5th in the 8-way.

Château D'Oex Hot Air Balloon Festival – Switzerland

After the World Championships closing ceremony, we received an impromptu invite to jump at the very first Hot Air Balloon Festival in Châteaux D'Oex in the Swiss Alps, which attracted hundreds of participants from around the globe. Annually, nearly one hundred hot-air balloons of all shapes, colours and sizes fill the skies, taking advantage of the exceptional winters, flying against the snow-capped alpine peaks and throughout the festival, which ran for a whole week, we skydived from balloons and the Pilatus Porter and watched other air enthusiasts demonstrating the skills in Para gliders, hang gliders, acrobatic planes and mini balloons. The panoramic Alpine views are just sensationally beautiful in the summer time, especially viewed from the silence of a hot air balloon basket, sailing above the lush green mountainside.

Shortly after our return to the UK, Symbiosis were awarded the Prince of Wales Cup and we attended the presentation ceremony in London to receive the cup from the Prince of Wales himself. What an amazing end to another amazing year!

In early 1980, Symbiosis were approached by a film producer, Julian Grant, to take part in a TV aerial extravaganza called The Great North Face Air Race. We snapped up the offer and on 18th March, Dave Waterman as cameraman, Rob, Geoff, William, Dane and myself flew out to Switzerland for a week, accommodated in a plush hotel in Grindlewald. Also staying at our hotel were other sporting experts invited to take part in the film/documentary with Per Lindstrand's balloon team, hot-dog skiers, husky teams, microlights and the film crew. At sparrow's fart each day, before the rest of the skiing population rose from their beds, we boarded a train which was scheduled especially for the film crew and us from Grindlewald station and travelled up the mountains to Kleine Scheidegg, taking in some of the most spectacular views for the forty (or so) minute journey. The next stop up from Kleine Scheidegg was the Jungfraujoch, so we took the opportunity to visit; the journey itself an awesome experience as seven out of the nine km track are in a tunnel that penetrates the heart of the Eiger and Monach mountains, twisting through solid cliff face and glacial ice. Throughout the following week, we just had a blast, skydiving out of the mountain rescue Llama helicopters and Pilatus Porter, the runway being the slopes of the Olympic Lauberhorn ski slope. The skydiving wasn't filmed in the sequence it was shown in the film; that was the editor's job to put each

With HRH Prince Charles

sporting element together to make it look like an air race. With two teams of red and blue, we exited the helicopters and skydived down the north face of the Eiger passing the baton to each other. One person from each team landed with precise accuracy next to a hot-dog skier, who skied down the mountainside passing the baton to the dog sled mushers, who raced their huskies across the mountain to the corresponding balloon team. Jumping in the Alps came with a few potential hazards and we took great care covering our equipment's handles, three-ring circus and pull-out Velcro when the helicopter came in to land besides us creating clouds of snow. Snow-dust on the metal parts of the rig froze solid at the high altitudes over the mountains, welding the metal 3-ring assembly together so we were constantly rotating the rings as we climbed to altitude, ensuring they would release if we needed to cut-away a malfunction. After completing ten jumps, our filming was in the can and while the other teams continued their race elements, we were free to ski our bums off taking advantage of the empty slopes at Kleine Scheidegg where, before sunrise, we had the whole mountain to ourselves.

Kings Island Theme Park, Cincinnati

If 1980 had started off well then it was to get even better with an invite to work in America by Paul McCowan, to be a member of his Firestone Skydiving Team in Cincinnati, Ohio. Dane, my long term boyfriend, accompanied me on the adventure and we set off for a new life in America where we rented a smart condominium in Wilmington, Ohio. The Firestone Team consisted of four skydivers, Paul, Dane, Craig Wilco and myself, a flying team with two biplanes and a hot-air balloon and crew. The show format started off each evening with a biplane dogfight over the Kings Island show ground, followed by the launching of a hot-air balloon from a small arena. The arena was our landing point, not much bigger than a boxing ring, situated in front of a restaurant and next to the water feature and 325ft tall Eiffel Tower. After a few thousand jumps of aiming for and landing on a circular 10cm target, a boxing ring offered me loads of breathing space. Within the theme park was a zoo and high-speed rides and apart from the designated landing area, there wasn't anywhere else to land, no overshoots or undershoots, unless that is, we fancied a tree landing in the dense woods, or in the wild animal park or lion enclosures. While the biplane dogfight took place, then pre-launch balloon inflation, four of us luxuriated in the Firestone DC3 fuselage watching the show unfold below. When Steve Adams

Firestone Team in DC3 door

launched the balloon and was out of the arena, we exited the aircraft overhead forming a four-way formation, spinning it like a carousel, then doing a bomb-burst made spectacular for the spectators with the trailing red smoke from our ankles. The Firestone Team put on a thrilling show each evening which was a huge crowd puller, especially, as the public remarked, as there was a 'girl' on the team. Each evening, after the show, we took advantage of jumping the queue on the theme rides and in particular The Beast roller-coaster, which when it opened in 1979, was the tallest, fastest, and longest wooden roller coaster in the world. It spanned about 35 acres and travelled through surrounding terrain deep into the woods and the ride itself lasted more than four minutes. What a perfect ending to a perfect day... It was a tough job, but someone had to do it!

Firestone Team jumping into Kings Island

On target

Apart from the Kings Island nightly shows, we also jumped into other demos, Evansville (Indiana), Middletown (Ohio), the Dayton Air Show, a night demo jump into Akron Hall of Fame, Whiteville, with an American football stuffed down my jumpsuit. The best demo while out there, was jumping into the USA National Championships in Richmond, Indiana where skydivers, unknown to each other, boarded the DC3 in Ohio, organised a 30-way hexa-wedge formation en-route in the aircraft and actually put the formation together in the sky, rotating five wedges back to another 30-way. What an ecstatic entrance to the championships, with everyone screaming and yahooing in freefall above the competitors on the DZ.

1980/1981

At the end of the demo season in Ohio, Dane and I drove south to Raeford, North Carolina, en-route to Zephyrhills where we'd arranged to join the Symbiosis clan and compete in the annual Turkey Meet in November. Arriving unannounced at Raeford wasn't a problem with Gene-Paul Thacker who always welcomed us wholeheartedly inviting us to dinner, cooked to perfection as always by his lovely wife, Miss Billy. For a week or so we hung out at the DZ, jumped with the locals, entered (and won gold medals as the Raeford Gang) an accuracy competition at Barnwell DZ and also did a few demos for Gene-Paul into a millionaire's party in Fayetteville and a night jump into Raeford stadium. With parting shots of "Y'all come back soon" from everyone on the DZ we set off on the 600 mile road trip in our not-so-trusty yellow Vega car to Zephyrhills Turkey Meet. The Meet was recognised as a major competition with world-class teams battling it out for trophies and celebrating Thanksgiving festivities and organised big-way multi-aircraft loads. The icing on the cake was we (Symbiosis and Friends, with special guest Joannie Murphy) won the 16-way event.

On a night jump with a full load in 40T DC3, as we approached 12,000ft, the aircraft had engine failure and everyone on board made a swift emergency exit. The terrain around Zephyrhills isn't the friendliest place for off-the-drop-zone-landings with tall pine trees and marshy swamps hosting well-camouflaged alligators and snakes in the limited night time light. The pilot (I think Val Thal was flying) made a successful landing and every skydiver survived to tell the tale, however the two people who had the misfortune to have malfunctions, survived to tell the tale but never saw their main canopies again.

During the winter of 1980, we went back to our day jobs to raise funds again for yet another 8-way training camp scheduled for a whole month commencing mid-May in Raeford, North Carolina. I found temporary secretarial work with Bosch in Farnborough who were most supportive, offering me work in all departments each and every time I returned from trips away and I also took on barmaid jobs at Pantiles and Ragamuffins in Camberley, where I worked long into the night and next mornings on Thursdays (grab a granny night) and Saturday and Sunday evenings. With so little sleep, I was like a walking zombie but I made a fortune in tips when customers offered me drinks and rather than rip them off with the full price of a drink (which I could easily have done),

I took just 50p and put it in my tips jar. I very much appreciated the tip and the customers appreciated I wasn't taking them for a ride.

Another major boost to my income came in March 1980 when the advertising agency for Guinness contacted me to do an advert, the theme being how Guinness enhanced a female's performance in their chosen field. We used Charlie Shea-Simonds' Stampe biplane for the advert and had to do about 8 jumps to get the exact shot but I wasn't complaining, as jumping from a bi-plane is a real treat that not many people get to experience. The reason we needed so many jumps was the photographer, although expert in his field, was filming from the chase aircraft and the non-sky-diving cameramen was not used to, and totally unnerved, when sitting in the open door when flying alongside us to get the shots he needed. We did offer the help of a skydiving cameraman to do the shots but they insisted they were OK to do it themselves. We eventually got the sky shots but then the pub shots of me drinking Guinness had to be done, so we took the crew to the Swan at Enford where we were all treated to a hearty meal and pints and pints of Guinness. What a bonus! I got to do the jumping from the biplane and along with the meal and liquid refreshments, my wallet was filled with a stash of skydiving money. I can't say the Guinness enhanced my skydiving at all, as drinking and skydiving don't go together, but I can vouch for the severe windy conditions later that evening when I must have blown a hole in the ozone layer!

Two more fantastic opportunities fell into Symbiosis' laps during mid-March with sponsorship from Heineken and an amazing offer to make another film/air race, a pilot series called Run the Gauntlet Alpine Challenge in the world capital of winter glitz, St Moritz, Switzerland. In the poshest of posh hotels, we rubbed shoulders with stratospherically rich clientele clad in Prada ski wear, meanwhile we wore hired ski suits from a shop in Bristol. The format for the pilot was the same as the previous Alpine Challenge in Grindlewald two years earlier and we were familiar with the film crew's requirements, so to us it was a busman's holiday in an exclusive ski resort. For a full week we skydived our bums off, jumping out of the mountain rescue Llama helicopters, Pilatus Porter and balloons and when we weren't required for filming, had the entire ski resort to explore, our passes giving us access to the winter sports available on the eponymous frozen lake, ice skating, horse racing, husky and sled racing and also the last remaining natural ski bob run in the world, the Cresta Run. Women are not allowed to participate in skeleton competition but I took the opportunity to sample part of the course, riding not in a toboggan but sitting on a large plastic carrier bag which was fast enough for me.

It was time to pack our bags and travel to North Carolina, our training camp on the USA Golden Knights' training drop zone, Raeford.

With a successful four-week training camp at an end, the local DZ jumpers asked us to join them in a 36-way out of the DC3 from 16,000ft. For a style and accuracy drop zone, it was a pretty impressive sight to see so many canopies in the air at the same time. Gene-Paul asked us also to jump into a demo at a pig roast at a nearby DZ at Derby and we jumped (no pun intended) at the opportunity, putting together an impromptu 23-way formation which we organised on the climb to altitude. The last and final jump before departing was a special request from Gene-Paul, who asked every female on the DZ to put together an 8-girl over his DZ as it had never been done before. We were all more than happy to oblige and from 11,000ft we exited the Beaver aircraft, formed a swift 8-girl star and for 6,000ft screamed and yelled until break-off. Gene-Paul was ecstatic and provided the DZ community with a free BBQ and beers all round. The girls on Raeford's first 8-way had four Brits in it, Glynis Howarth, Kath McCormack, Esther Reynolds and myself, one Canadian soldier Eileen Vaughan, the others from USA, Lori, Dawn and Rayleen.

On our return to the UK, the National Championships took place at Netheravon with all events, RW and Style and Accuracy during the one week. The championships attracted the largest attendance ever at a Nationals with over 140 entries. 9 eight way teams, 25 four way teams, 55 individual accuracy entries and 55 style entries. Symbiosis had an excellent meet achieving 1st place in both 8-way and 4-way being selected to represent Great Britain again at Zephyrhills later in the year. To top off winning the 8-way, I also came first in lady's accuracy, first in lady's style and first lady overall.

So, 1981 was a bumper year for me, taking part in a British 24-man formation over Bembridge Air Show, Isle of Wight and also qualified to represent GB at World Meets in both classics and RW in the same year. The classics World Cup in Style and Accuracy, was in Graz, Austria throughout August and competing again 33 other countries, I claimed Silver, jumping my Pegasus canopy only missing out on the gold by three dirty little centimetres. The helmet number 'draw' found a victim for number 13. SCOTTY! He preferred to call it 12a but it still proved to be unlucky for him. After two rounds of Accuracy the lads were sitting pretty good with Scotty Milne 0.00 and 0.01, Dave Tylcoat 0.02 and 0.00, Steve Treble 0.05 and 0.07, and Jim Coffey on 0.00 and 0.00. Then came the crunch for Scotty's ankle. After his first Style jump he landed with a whump, Harry Stoofers, and that was the end of his competition.

Later that year Symbiosis flew from the UK to California for another training camp at Perris Valley, California in preparation for the World Championships in Zephyrhills, Florida later in October. At the end of the training camp, the team had five days to chill out before flying to Florida and William casually mentioned he would like to BASE jump from El Capitan. BASE is an acronym that stands for four categories of fixed objects to jump from, Building, Antenna, Span and Earth, and due to the usually lower altitudes was considered significantly more dangerous than skydiving from an aircraft. That said, launching from the top of El Capitan offered a higher platform to jump from than any of the parachute displays I'd jumped into over London, where air clearance was no higher than 1500ft due to the close proximity of London airports. BASE jumping at the time was frowned upon by the British Parachute Association and anyone found to have done one, was outlawed from the Association, banned, resulting in never being able to skydive out of an aircraft in the UK again. I didn't take too much persuading to agree and before I knew it, I was in a hire car with Dane, Robin Mills, Geoff Sanders and William, beginning an eight-hour overnight journey to Yosemite National Park.

Five hours into the overnight journey, William pulled up outside a bar in what looked a quiet neighbourhood for a comfort break and caffeine injection. We piled out of the vehicle and headed towards the flashing neon lights of a corner cafe/bar, laughing and chatting excitedly as we pushed through the doors. The establishment was a real dive and as the door closed behind us, the bartender was the first to see us, then the place fell silent and everyone in the room stared at us. The people standing against the walls watched us as we bravely (or stupidly) walked towards the only empty table and the men playing pool interrupted their game to size us up. Seriously out of our comfort zone in one of those 'Oh Shit!' moments, we sensed we were about as welcome as a fart in a space-suit. We should have left but were far too scared to turn around and head for the exit.

Our saving grace was William's nervous gibbering in his polite and posh English accent which softened the hostile atmosphere when the waitress at our table shouted out, "Oh my! Y'all from England? Ah jes love your accent!" She became our protector, like a mother hen fussing around us asking us to 'say something' and although we made our coffee order with her, none of us dared to use the bathrooms. We drank our coffees quickly and stood up to leave, William placing a large tip on the waitress's plate and in silence with every set of eyes watching, we walked towards the exit fully expecting to be jumped on.

I held my breath and as soon as we were outside, we ran like the clappers towards our hire car, dived inside then screeched off into the night as fast as the wheels could go.

As we approached Yosemite Valley, we stared wide-eyed in awe as creeping light spread through mist and treetops giving us the most magical welcome. The breath-taking vision emerging before our eyes was majestic, soaring cliffs where light and shadows danced on the granite, the imposing face of Half Dome, trickling waterfalls, canyons and giant Sequoia reaching hundreds of feet into the vivid blue skies. I thought I'd died and gone to heaven!

At the base of El Capitan's granite vertical monolith face, we stood in the meadow looking up to the summit some 3,000ft (about 900m) above and wished we were at the top looking down.

In front of us a lay an arduous ten miles and six to eight-hour trek up steep, sometimes rocky avalanched slopes to reach the top and vital to our successful ascent, we stocked up with energy foods and water to prevent dehydration. We not only faced the physical challenge but also the risk of encountering one or more of the park's black bears in the wilderness, so our food was kept in bear resistant containers. We discussed all the risks, the most forefront in our minds of course was one of adverse weather and reaching the top and not being able to jump. If wind strength was too high and blowing towards the granite face, or the cloud base was below the launch point, we faced the lengthy trek back down again. Ideally, we hoped for nil to light winds and the descent to the valley floor would take only seconds in freefall, followed by a couple of minutes under the canopy.

At eight o'clock that morning, we headed off on the trail out of Yosemite Valley close to the spectacular Yosemite Falls which is the highest measured waterfall in North America. The upper Falls plunge 1,430ft to the middle cascades where the Falls hurl themselves again with sensational and deafening force for a further 675ft. The lower Falls, the final 320ft drop, spilled into the plunge pool at Yosemite Creek and flowed into the nearby Merced River. We stopped and stared in awe at its beauty for a while, wishing we could stay longer but with a very long day ahead, had to keep moving on our upwards and westward climb. Geoff noticed an enormous tree stump from a felled giant sequoias and used it as a ramp to practice his launch from the edge of the rock, 3,200ft above us. His efforts were in vain but I will tell you about what happened when he actually jumped from the ledge off El Cap, later in the chapter.

The paths and tracks throughout the Yosemite Valley were not as established as they are today and the lack of footfall made the climb very strenuous for me. The difficulty varied dramatically with occasional scrambling over loose rocks and slippery boulders, the aftermath of avalanches, where the odd leg-up and holding on to each other was essential to continue. Sharp limestone covered the route which involved some serious Mark-1 scrambling and white-knuckle death grips. Falling was not an option, it would most definitely have caused serious bodily harm, not just because of the fall but because it would have been broken by an unfriendly and spiky cactus or two on the descent. At some stages the cactus and low shrubs scratched and tore at our legs but there were many other paths of rock that allowed ease of ascent.

Out of necessity, we stopped occasionally to take in essential food, drinking litres of water to keep the energy levels up and avoid dehydration. The cotton top I wore was soaked in sweat, as wet as if I'd dived into a swimming pool fully clothed, and frequently I removed it from my back to wring out and dry out on a hot granite slab for a few minutes in the searing heat. The trail wasn't always visible either, hidden by overgrown shrubbery and grasses or a huge fallen tree, which we were challenged to scramble over, and then forever questioning if we were heading in the right direction. Carrying my heavy parachuting equipment just about finished me off physically; the exertion and lack of oxygen at the increasing altitude affected my breathing and for every step, I took my ribcage convulsed, stomach retched and I experienced an overwhelming giddiness and light-headedness bordering on fainting. Towards the summit the steep trail was surrounded by huge rocks and boulders, some of which had natural geometric faces with eyes appearing to follow my every move as I edged past, or perhaps maybe I was hallucinating.

During the final stages of the climb, I ignored the awesome views emerging before me focussing instead on placing one foot in front of the other and after much plodding, we reached the top. Physically drained, I was in a state of euphoric bliss, overcome emotionally and relieved to have reached the top; at once I removed and laid down the parachuting equipment which had left deep welt marks on my shoulders. We'd made it!

Earlier that morning, whilst on the ground looking up El Capitan's towering rock-face, I imagined the summit had a flat top but from where I was standing it had a wavy shape, like a wedge, with one low side and one very sharp edge. Standing on an enormous boulder there was absolutely nothing higher than me; to my left a magnificent view of Half Dome with its sheer cliff face reaching

5,000ft above the Yosemite Valley floor. Beyond Half Dome the snow-capped mountain tops pointed majestically into the wide blue skies in the distance. In front, the valley floor, the Merced River running through the meadows, woodland and valley below. Nothing could have prepared me for the visual sensory overload experience of being immersed in such natural grandeur. It was breathtakingly beautiful, magical, mystical, magnificent and surreal.

A short distance further down the trail, we retreated into some trees to repack our parachutes. One of the risks after jumping from the top was if the parachute involuntarily turned 180 degrees on opening, it would fly straight towards and into the sheer granite face. In the perfect world, the parachute should open facing on heading away from the rock face, if it flew towards the rock and hit it, then the chances of it inflating and flying again were slim to no chance.

We opened our containers, shook and aired the parachutes removing sand and grit picked up on the dusty Perris Valley drop zone floor, neatly folded and closed the parachute containers again securing closed with the pin. William was renowned for being the untidiest parachute packer in the universe (OK, I exaggerate for effect) and repacked his rig again and again until he was sufficiently satisfied that it should open and fly straight.

Yosemite Valley with El Capitan and Half Dome

The location where we repacked our parachutes was a few hundred feet higher than the ledge we were to launch from, so as the sun lowered, towards sunset, we made our way gingerly down the steep granite slope. The decline was so steep and for fear of breaking into an involuntary run, I skidded down on my backside, the rubber soles of my trainers screeching like tyres in the generated heat. Our altimeters read approximately 3,200ft above the valley which was comforting, knowing we could get a good ten to twelve seconds freefall and fly our bodies away from the rock face to open our parachutes around 1500ft.

The weather conditions were favourable to jump and we watched the setting sun colour the opposing valley walls into a vivid orangey-red before tall shadows crept slowly up the walls until there was no sunlight left at all. We tossed a coin to decide which order to jump, at which stage there was no other option but to jump. Had the weather conditions not been favourable, the only other way down would have resulted in a four or five-hour trek, a daunting task without torches, ambient light and the unfortunate encounter with an angry bear!

We staggered the launch to allow a good ten seconds time delay between each person, William went first followed by Geoff, Robin, me, then Dane. In a line we leaned against the boulder behind us to allow as long a run-up to the edge, then joined hands in a final team handshake. After all of Geoff's practice from the Giant Sequoia tree stump he tripped on a small stone and as he went over the edge went unstable and tumbled for quite some time before stabilising out to deploy his parachute.

It was my turn. I leaned backwards against the rock as if awaiting a race starter gun fire, then sprinted forward lunging outward with arms extended high in front of me awaiting the big unknown. Without the speed of an aircraft's slipstream, I tipped into a head-down diving position where I came face-to-face with the vastness of the sheer granite wall. In slow motion I heard the word "WOW" escape my mouth and as I glanced left and right was engulfed in the amazing vision of El Capitan's gigantic structure. My downward speed increased and I tracked away from the granite wall for all I was worth, glanced down at the giant green trees below and saw the small specks of colour below being William's and Robin's parachutes opened parachutes. I deployed my pilot chute and immediately, before the canopy had broken free from the bag, took hold of the risers in anticipation of my canopy turning towards the rock face. My canopy opened perfectly and breathless, I inhaled to the end of my tippy toes and my entire body buzzed with adrenalin like never before.

Behind me I heard loud yahooing which echoed down the valley below and glancing around, I noticed a group of climbers set up in their Bivouacs on the rock face preparing to sleep for the night before continuing the following day on their climb to the summit. The visuals for them watching us falling past them with a galaxy of stars as a backdrop must have been incredible, as exciting for them to watch as it was for us to freefall past them.

Under the canopy I became immediately aware of the strength of wind blowing towards me, so strong there was no forward penetration and in fact I was edging slowly backwards towards the rock face. There was nothing I could do but pull down on my front risers hoping to edge forward but to no avail, I just hung there, totally at the fate of that wind. At about 600ft the winds decreased quite significantly and my canopy surged forward to make good headway towards the landing area. I lifted up my legs to decrease any drag and steered towards a sandy bank on the far side of the Merced River and nestled between the trees where my accuracy experience came in very handy. In near darkness and below the tree line the wind was non-existent, not a breath, and my canopy surged forward at a great rate of knots towards the ground and with full brakes applied, I stoofed-in unceremoniously doing a skidding nine-yard PLF.

Daylight quickly dissolved into darkness and I heard rustling in the trees, something big was approaching and surely I was going to be attacked by a bear. In complete darkness William's clipped English accent was music to my ears when he courteously offered to take my kit off, whilst giggling like an innocent schoolboy. To this day, William's claim to fame is that he took my kit off in the wilderness of the Yosemite Valley. We made our way to the Yosemite Lodge bar where the others were awaiting our arrival and, with no means whatsoever of communication with each other, had an anxious half hour wait for Dane to return. I doubt any of us can remember much about the rest of the evening which blurred away in the richest concoction of elation, adrenalin and alcohol but forever etched in my mind is the memory of one of the most amazing experiences of my entire life.

JSPC(N) – 1983

At that time, I was employed at the Joint Service Parachute Centre at Netheravon working with another of my most-fantastic bosses, Major Gerry O'Hara MBE. Gerry had previously been my Red Devil Team Commander after Major Schofield left the team and his out-of-the-blue telephone call inviting me to work alongside him at the parachute centre at Netheravon didn't take too much thinking about. "Ummmmm, let me think about this! Yes! Most definitely! When do you want me to start?"

I moved to Wiltshire and bought a house in Durrington village, just a few miles from the DZ, and apart from sleeping and storing my clothes there, I mostly spent 18 hours a day, every day, at the drop zone. Employed as instructors and junior staff at the parachute centre were some of the most amazing people I have ever worked with. There were members from every service, Army, Royal Marines, Navy, Air Force with individuals from Parachute Regiment, Scottish Regiments, Royal Artillery, REME, RAF, Royal Engineers and a Territorial Army soldier, Apples Applegate to name a long standing member. What a hoot those years were. Everyone who worked there, without fail, had the most excellent work ethic pulling together as a well-oiled team to keep the centre running efficiently usually from well before first light every day, until well after the sun had gone to bed. The reward to everyone after the last parachute was packed was to down some well-earned refreshing beers and relive a few stories from the day's events in the bar which Gerry O'Hara made with his own fair hands. I cherished the social life on the DZ and most weekends was party, party, party with fancy dress, BBQs and beer fights with Geordie Laing and Bob Charters.

I worked in the office, the engine room as we referred to it, administering everything and anything from answering the phone; organising the military's adventure training courses; ordering parts for the aircraft; restocking the bar; managing the parachute shop; manifesting; selling jump tickets; bar maid; chief cook and bottle washer; instructing; coaching; parachute packing; driver; book-keeper; banker; and sometimes a sympathetic shoulder to a struggling skydiver, dishing out encouragement and advice.

The Army Parachute Association worked alongside the Joint Service Parachute Centre as agent (they owned the aircraft and equipment and hired it out to the JSPC) but they, at the time, only had one office employee, secretary being Major (Ret'd) Donald Scarfe. I took on all the APA administrative work as well as the

JSPC course work too as Donald didn't have anyone to help him. The task was enormous but between us, we kept the ship afloat running both organisations side by side successfully. The JSPC and APA offices were the engine rooms and Gerry, Donald and myself were the oily rags keeping everything running smoothly. At Netheravon, I had the privilege of working with some of the most amazing Commandants, APA Secretaries, Centre Chief Instructors and Sergeant Majors over the years, keeping an extremely efficient and safe parachuting operation in motion.

One of my regular office tasks was to order and replenish the Parachute Centre's stationery, stores items, aircraft parts and toiletries. Every month I did a massive stationery order through the MOD's purchasing system and for about twelve years, the orders were pretty repetitive when I used and updated the previous order inserting only the current dates. Early one sunny morning, a huge lorry with equally huge trailer container pulled up outside my airfield office and the driver dismounted his cabin. I escorted him into the centre's storeroom and asked if he could put the delivery in there. He took off his cap, scratched his head before laughing out loud advising that the storeroom wasn't big enough for the order. He then asked if some of the staff could assist him unload as everything he carried on both the lorry and container was for the parachute centre. Apart from two or three small boxes containing small stationery items, the rest was toilet rolls on large pallets. The staff obliged and helped unload from the lorry palette after palette and when the packing hall was nearly full to the rafters, Skippy Morris and Paul Applegate asked how many more palettes were for the centre. The driver said, "All of it mate! All 250,000 toilet rolls!"

It was a massive error on my behalf, I must have leaned on the zero button which added a few more to the original order. It was a memorable mistake, the day still etched in the forefront of everyone's mind who was there to witness my error. The driver didn't want to return the toilet rolls as it entailed too much paperwork (no pun intended) for him to fill in so, as the loo rolls continued to be unloaded, the staff stacked them in the ground training room reaching nearly to the roof. It was hilarious as there was hardly any space left in the hangar to pack parachutes.

I was baffled why the MOD hadn't questioned the unusually high demand for toilet rolls, so got straight on the blower to ask why. The polite chap in the MOD stores said that because we ran an adventure training centre with what they considered to be fearful and high risk activities, he assumed the students attending the courses would be crapping themselves and didn't query the extra volume in order. It goes without saying we didn't need to order loo rolls for a very long time and neither did the surrounding army units of Support Weapons Wing and 656 Army Air Corps, who all came and took some away vast quantities for their stores.

Having had the opportunity to write these memoirs I couldn't leave out one of the funniest blokes to ever cross my path, Kev Waterhouse. He came to the JSPC staff as an instructor on loan from The Parachute Regiment having served on the Red Devils for a few years and he immediately struck a chord with everyone he met with his unforgettable cheeky schoolboy antics. At staff BBQs he'd remove the baby beetroot from the jars and replace with round, black BBQ coals and unsuspecting diners got the shock of their lives when they tried to eat it. I know a certain Glitter chap is in the confines of HM prison now but Kev had his act down to a 'T' and entertained everyone in the bar dressed in his platform shoes, tight lycra leggings and spikey wig where everyone chanted loudly they wanted to be in his gang. He'd be forever sneaking up behind me inserting his wet finger into my ear hole (I'm assuming it was his finger!) and when I was expecting visitors in my office, he'd open the door, enter, let off a silent but deadly fart and leave, closing the door behind him. I was left with a foul smelling office and very red face trying to convince my visitors the smell wasn't me. He pinged bungies at my backside at the very moment I was closing my parachute container and I lost count of the times he told me to pull his finger saying "Go on! You know you want to!" He was such a rascal, but a loveable rascal and everyone appreciated his banter and sense of humour.

Major O'Hara used to organise regular night jumps for Friday or Saturday nights when there was a full moon and due to complaints of aircraft noise from the local villagers the briefing was strict... he emphasised quite categorically there was to be no yahooing in freefall or when under the canopy. We checked the weather conditions, wind direction and strength with the local Met Office and the exit and opening point was towards the village of Netheravon. When the moon was high and bright in the sky, I took off on the first lift and jumped with Gerry O'Hara, Pete Lambson and John Horne. We landed in the pit where a parked Landrover shone its headlights into wind to give everyone the direction of landing and a view of the ground.

Kev was on the second lift and asked me to stay in the pit to watch him do his first night accuracy approach. I watched the aircraft lights flashing overhead on jump run, then the engines cut back and although I couldn't see anyone in freefall due to darkness, I could hear the distinct noise of skydivers in freefall. The crack of canopies filled the air but then I heard another flapping sound, one of a canopy snivelling and streaming at 120mph. It was Kev with his first night jump malfunction. The air was blue, filled with Kev's broad Yorkshire accent cursing and swearing, calling his canopy all the names under the sun. After a brief time, I heard the loud crack of his reserve opening and Kev continued to swear, effing and blinding until a short time later, in the darkness behind me I heard a 'whooomp' as he stoofed in. His very Yorkshire "Fuckin 'ell!" announced his landing. It was pitch black and impossible for him to see the ground come up to meet him and fortunately he was ok but his wallet was about to take a severe battering. We couldn't locate his main canopy however, which although had cyalume glow sticks tied to the risers, wasn't found til the next day. By the time we walked back to the parachute centre, I think every resident in the local village had telephoned the parachute centre to complain not about the aircraft noise but the loud swearing in the skies above their homes. That was the end of night jumps at Netheravon for quite a while and Kev not only had to get the beers in for his first night jump, but also his first night jump malfunction.

Working at Netheravon was a dream, fun job, where it was a laugh a minute with the best people anyone could wish to work with. My office had a view of the manifest hut, the aircraft and the vastness of Salisbury Plain. I admit to sneaking out the office every single good weather day to do a few jumps and never getting around to logging most of them as it was always a case of "Oh, I'll do it later!" and then never did get around to it. The quality and amount of skydivers jumping at Netheravon throughout the 80s and 90s afforded everyone to make up fun (and serious) teams which we entered in competitions throughout the UK and RAPA (Germany) resulting in many wins in all disciplines. More than anything I enjoyed giving back to the sport, by coaching in any way I could in accuracy, skydiving and packing parachutes and I've lost count of the jumps I was base for the student to pin me. More often than not the students were blokes and I rewarded each and every one of them with a kiss pass which besides relaxing them, put a smile on their face, before continuing with the planned flying exercises. Every skydiver attempted accuracy in the 70s and 80s with varying levels of success as most canopies gave a reasonably controlled approach and competitions usually had huge attendance. However, the demise of the accuracy event in the UK came with the release of smaller, lightweight and faster flying canopies that don't offer slow approaches and descent to the target for precise foot placement on the tiny 2cm target. The accuracy event is huge in Europe so hopefully it will make a big comeback in the UK one day.

RAPA and Commonwealth Games 1986

After competing and winning the overall accuracy and 4-way at the RAPA (Bad Lippspringe, Germany) Championships with my civilian team 'Going South', with Kelvin White, Mark Rodwell (Rodders) and Barry Large, I flew from Germany, compliments of the BBC, to Edinburgh, Scotland. Simon Ward and The Royal Marines Freefall Team met me at the airport and together we drove further north to the Royal Marines' base at Arbroath. Stuart Morris, head of BBC, had asked me the previous year if I would jump into and open the 1986 Commonwealth Games in Meadowbank Stadium Edinburgh. His plan was for me to be escorted into the arena by the Royal Marines Team, most of who worked alongside me at the Joint Service Parachute Centre. Special parachutes were ordered for the event; the 'Royals' had the Union Flag design on both the underneath and top surfaces of their canopies, and my parachute had the flag of Scotland, the Saltire, St Andrew's cross. The organisers arranged for one practice jump into an empty Meadowbank stadium using our own equipment and on that occasion the weather was beautiful, with wall-to-wall blue skies and light winds in a direction free from any obstacles to cause turbulence when flying into the arena. Flying over Edinburgh in the Sea King helicopter was amazing, with aerial views of Arthur's Seat, Holyrood Park, lochs, golf courses and standing majestically in the distance, Edinburgh Castle. It was such a clear day, the skies free of pollution and with crystal clear views in the far distance of the Forth Bridge.

The practice jump went according to plan, the Royal Marines who, incidentally, are World Champions and World Record holders in Canopy Relative Work, landed their stacked parachutes into the arena, escorting me into the arena to land last. We then drove the two-hour journey to Arbroath, where the new and unassembled parachuting equipment to be used at the opening ceremony was in boxes awaiting us. We spent the next day assembling the equipment and the canopies had to be jumped initially at sub-terminal speeds to stretch the lines, not causing any damage to the canopies, and to test out the flying characteristics. New parachutes tended to open hard and fast causing the parachutist's body to 'slump' downwards into the harness, sometimes causing whiplash and to the male species amongst us, crushed nuts (and I am not referring to those bought in 100g packets in the supermarket). When the equipment was assembled to our personal flight settings, we boarded the Sea King helicopter, climbed to about 5,000ft above the ground and exited in sequence, each deploying our parachutes after three to five seconds. The test jumping proved a huge 'fail' when five of the new parachutes split their seams on opening, resulting in each jumper cutting away the trash above their heads and deploying reserve parachutes.

For the next day or two, we spent our time repairing the canopies and repacking reserve parachutes whilst reasoning why the parachutes had split and discussing options to minimise any further damage. The Union Flag and St Andrew's cross 'skin' on the under-side of the canopies was made of zero porosity material which had the texture of Walker's crisp packets and when the air hit the canopy, the parachute cells ripped and lines snapped where they joined the canopy. It was obvious we would have to do some parachute packing modifications in an attempt to slow down the opening sequence and again we boarded the Sea King, climbed to altitude and exited into the slipstream, intending to take the parachutes to terminal velocity of 120 miles per hour. I deployed my pilot chute and winced in anticipation of the hard opening. I was not wrong in my expectations and the canopy opened so hard, with a 'wham' I thought I'd hit the ground and for a few seconds saw stars. My canopy remained intact but all around me others were experiencing malfunctions, broken lines and torn canopies resulting in more cutaways and reserve deployments.

On the third practice day, we made a decision to pack the parachutes one final time in preparation for a low parachute display into the Meadowbank Stadium when our intention was to deploy immediately after leaving the helicopter door and hopefully not put any more undue stress on them. On the actual show day, we climbed aboard the Sea King with our in-air cameraman Simon Ward who, wearing incredibly heavy camera equipment on his helmet, ran the risk of breaking his neck should his parachute open sharply. The cameras Simon used transmitted live in-air footage directly from the helicopter, in freefall and also under his deployed parachute to the BBC, thus enabling TV viewers to watch everything in real time as it happened, which was the first time this had ever been done.

Fully kitted up and ready to emplane, we checked the weather forecast and although the fair weather and blue skies in Arbroath offered good parachuting conditions, we were advised that the weather forecast for Edinburgh was worsening with torrential rain, gale force winds and low cloud on its way. As we flew overhead from Arbroath towards Edinburgh's skyline, it was obvious to us all the show was going to be a very low one indeed and regardless of the weather the show had to go ahead. The pilot flew the helicopter under the cloud base barely touching 900ft on our altimeters and the rain sprayed from the spinning rotor blades above us. We made eye contact with each other disguising any admission to being apprehensive about the weather conditions. Personally, I was absolutely bricking it but there was no way I was going to put my hand up and declare I didn't want to jump. Ideally, we needed the helicopter to gain altitude to 2,000ft but as we circled over the stadium, it was obvious that we wouldn't gain another inch of altitude, let alone another 1,000ft. That show had to go on and with 102 million viewers worldwide awaiting the union flag canopies escorting my Scottish Saltire canopy fly into the stadium, not jumping wasn't an option.

We circled low over the stadium trying to scrape some extra altitude and meanwhile watched the colourful opening ceremony displays taking place beneath us. The pilot shouted, "Clear to drop" and then proceeded on jump-run underneath the black, rain-filled cloud-base. Passing over the stadium towards our exit point, the pilot went into a steep climb into the patchy murk around us attempting to gain some extra space between us and the ground. One by one, the Royal Marines launched from the door disappearing in the slipstream behind the helicopter. I won't say at what altitude we left the helicopter, but none of us died and we all lived to tell the tale.

Last to exit, I deployed my parachute immediately out the door and as expected it slammed open, hard and fast and with much relief, was totally intact without any broken lines or canopy tears. Picking up my bearings I located the stadium in the distance, applied the brakes on my parachute to stay aloft for as long as I possibly could to allow the Royal Marines to spiral down and land before me. The winds were borderline(ish) and disconcertingly blowing in a direction over the grandstand towards the arena, creating dirty, turbulent air above the landing area. Turning my canopy into wind to face the grandstand, the air felt uncomfortably bumpy, my canopy was bucking like a bronco then deflated, folding into a bow configuration above my head. With little to no lift, I rapidly descended backwards, the canopy swinging me like a pendulum until I hit the deck like a sack of potatoes in the middle of the stadium.

The crowd gave a loud collective gasp, thinking I was injured and remained silent for what seemed a lifetime but in reality only a split second. When I jumped to my feet and brushed myself down, the crowd erupted into relieved applause and cheering. So hard was my landing the Royal Marines thought I'd broken my back and ran towards me initially to assist. When they realised I was OK, they picked me up and placed me on their shoulders while I waved ceremoniously to the crowds before sprinting quickly to do a team line-up in front of His Royal Highness, Prince Philip. Once outside the immediate stadium and into the service area, we dismantled the parachuting equipment and each and every parachute was ditched in a huge bin by the stadium exit. There was certainly no place for them in the skies above our or anybody else's heads and there was no better place for them than the trash bin.

During the weeks prior to flying to Scotland, I'd competed at The Rhine Army Parachuting Championships in Germany and throughout the entire competition I experienced a general feeling of sickness, spending most mornings throwing up outside my tent door. Other competitors witnessing my retching accused me of partying too hard the previous night but I didn't drink a drop throughout the competition due to taking medication for a heavy cold. It wasn't until after I returned home to Wiltshire, that I discovered I was four months pregnant with my first son, Scott. It's so cool to think my unborn son had accompanied me throughout the competition (which my team, Going South, won) and also into the spectacular opening ceremony at the Commonwealth Games. I doubt many can claim to have inherited the thrill-seeking gene from their mum at such an amazing event while still in foetus form and fortunately for him (and me) he suffered no side effects or injury from my hard landing.

Throughout my first pregnancy, my husband was a serving member of the Parachute Regiment and he was called away on military training exercises for the majority of my confinement leaving me, myself and I to get on with everything as normal. As secretary at the Joint Services Parachute Centre, I continued to work full time until the day before my son, Scott, was born. Doing packing checks and helping the students on with their equipment was a little bit cumbersome considering the size of my baby bump, but life went on as normal. I was secure in the knowledge that the Centre Sergeant Major, Royal Marine Pete Lambson, would taxi me to the hospital in the DZ pick-up truck should I go into labour. I finished work on Thursday, 26th February 1987 and the DZ staff had a usual staff get-together in the bar to celebrate three birthdays, Donald Scarfe, Keith Skelley and also Pete Lambson and little did I know that the following day, I'd be celebrating my own son's arrival.

When I gave birth to Scott, my husband was unreachable in the snowy wilderness of the Norwegian training area on a NATO AMFL exercise. Eventually, word got through to him and he arrived at my bedside at Salisbury District Hospital three days after Scott's birth and only then was I allowed to go home. His visit was very short-lived however and after three days at home, he returned to Norway and joined the rest of the battalion for the final part of the exercise. During the first year of Scott's life, my husband was away from home for forty weeks due to military exercises and without any family close-by, my life was that of a single parent to Scott and later Ross throughout most of my marriage. As spearhead infantry, The Parachute Regiment were never posted to exotic places but rather carried out six month tours to war-torn locations therefore families didn't get to live anywhere other than Aldershot, Bulford or Northern Ireland. As a military wife in Northern Ireland, I enjoyed the location enormously taking the children out to discover beautiful country parks, forests, castles, lochs and beaches and of course jump at the parachute centre at Ballykelly. My marriage didn't last however, but that wasn't as a result of the military taking him away. When I married, I thought I was my husband's bag for life but that wasn't to be. Moving swiftly on then!

My sons thoroughly enjoyed growing up at the parachute centre at Netheravon where the all-male military staff from various regiments took on the roles of older brothers, typically playing football or volley ball with them during their breaks from parachute training. When Scott and Ross were old enough to attend Netheravon Airfield playschool located at the bottom of the camp, I enjoyed an element of freedom again indulging in the odd staff jump every day.

On one occasion when my children were at playschool, I emplaned with seven other staff members, the aircraft wheels lifting off at around 11am which would, on any other occasion, allow ample time to climb to altitude, jump, land and pack my parachute before picking up the boys at 12 noon. At 3,000ft the pilot advised us skydivers in the back of the aircraft we were being held off by Air Traffic Control as fighter jets flying out of Boscombe Down were doing circuits over Netheravon Airfield's air space. This meant we couldn't fly over the drop zone and jump until air traffic confirmed to our pilot we were clear to drop. The pilot circled the aircraft above Sidbury Hill (near Tidworth) remaining at the same altitude ensuring we didn't encroach into the fighter jets' airspace, meanwhile everyone on board loosened parachute harnesses enabling us to stretch out and relax during the hold off. As time went on, I was all too aware that we might be airborne for an indefinite period of time and if we didn't jump soon, I wouldn't be at the Playschool to pick up my boys at 12 noon. We circled for ages and with relief the air traffic control gave us the 'clear to drop' instruction bang on noon and rather than climb to altitude, I asked the pilot to fly on run-in and let me jump out on a climbing pass over the playschool while the remaining staff on board continued their climb up to 12,000ft where they jumped without me. Descending under my opened parachute, I flew towards the playschool and landed directly in front of its entrance to a barrage of banter from bemused mums and dads who had used more conventional methods of transport pushing strollers and pushchairs to pick up their children. They nonchalantly rolled their eyes, feigned yawning and boredom while taunting me for being such a big time show-off, asking why I had to be different and why didn't I pick up my children in the normal way. Silly me, I thought everyone dropped in by parachute to pick up their children!

Motherhood is by far the biggest accomplishment in my life, far outweighing any skydiving achievements I've notched up. I just loved becoming a mother with babies who swathed me in unconditional love. Until the age of 34, my every day had been full-on skydiving and travel with no-one else to think about but myself. I lived skydiving, dreamed skydiving, ate skydiving, drank skydiving, my life was totally consumed with skydiving then suddenly, instead of packing parachutes I was packing nappies and with the same consequence. Get it wrong and believe me, they both open like a bag of shit! Scott and Ross watched me skydive on a daily basis so they weren't really fazed by it and neither impressed because parachuting was part of their daily scene and was the norm. I mean, isn't everyone's mum an ex-Red Devil, world champion who works at a parachute centre and skydives for a living? It was only when they were older and did their first skydive themselves, that my street-cred rocketed to the outer stratosphere and they then realised their mum really did have a life after all, other than being the good cop/bad cop in their lives.

Now that I'm a grandmother, Granny Smith, I'm pretty content with what life has thrown at me and I look forward to the day I can introduce the grand-children to skydiving in the indoor wind tunnel and perhaps inject them with adrenaline, turn on the magic, and start them on an epic journey through life like mine. I exchanged fashion, fancy clothes and flashy cars for parachutes, ripcords and altimeters where my every day dress code was jumpsuit and helmet. There are no strangers in skydiving and everyone is on the same level regardless of ability, wealth or background and I've made wonderful, long-standing friendships with some amazing people, travelling far and wide to skydive in the skies around the world.

If you asked me what has been the best part of my life, my answer would be absolutely, every single part of it! My most memorable jump? There are too many to choose from, but one particularly visually memorable jump was a 3-way with Kelvin White and Barry Large, my Going South team mates, over Netheravon Airfield. We'd returned to our home drop zone after a competition at another location and decided to do a fun jump to finish the weekend off. It was a bitterly cold day with wall-to-wall blue skies, and a temperature of -25 degrees at 16,000ft where we huddled together in the back of the aircraft freezing, not having inflight doors at the time. We exited the aircraft and performed a few quick formations, then became distracted by the glittering effect of millions of tiny diamonds, diamond dust, flashing around us in freefall, the phenomenon caused when tiny crystals, tumbling through the air, reflected sunlight into our eyes. Without any communication, all three of us abandoned our planned skydive, mouthed "Wow" to each other and enjoyed the surrounding glittery visuals similar, I can only imagine, to being inside a glitter globe. Had it not been for our audible alarms beeping in our ears alerting us to our break-off and pull altitude and bringing us back to reality, we may well have remained in the magic glitter globe forever more.

Hall of Fame Inductee
with John Smyth and Pat Thomas

In 1998, I was awarded the Royal Aero Club Gold Medal at a ceremony in London for my achievements in skydiving joining the ranks of Bleriot, The Wright Brothers and De Havilland and recently was inducted into the Skydiving Hall of Fame in Chicago, USA 2013. I have my good friends Pat Thomas of Sun Path Products and Larry Bagley (USPA) to thank for nominating and supporting me wholeheartedly in the first instance, and to everyone else involved, for their overwhelming vote of acceptance as a Hall of Fame inductee. To the BPA, thank you for assisting my travel to the USA to receive the accolade without which I wouldn't have been able to attend. Being inducted into the Hall of Fame in front of an audience of skydiving legends, most of whom I've grown up in the sport with throughout the world, was the icing on my cake. John Smyth gave me an amazing introduction, highlighting my career before I was presented with the Hall of Fame blazer which I wear with enormous pride. It is ok to go to bed in a Hall of Fame Blazer isn't it? Icing doesn't come any thicker than that and I am so proud and honoured to have received such an accolade.

Special thanks to Colonel Ed Gardener for his first-hand knowledge of the Red Devils' history and also his kind words in my foreword. Thanks also to James F. Curtis III (Curt) for filling in the gaps in my recollection of Hotel California, Pope Valley, and to Grant Meekey aka The Wookie, for his persistence, nudging me on and encouraging me to write my memoirs. This book wouldn't have happened if it wasn't for the help Dougie Peacock has given me. Dougie has known me throughout my skydiving career in his capacity as RAF military skydiver, world class competitor, world class judge and world class coach. His advice getting these memoirs printed has been invaluable, as has his encouragement when in despair I nearly threw in the towel, believing no-one would be interested in reading my story. Thank you also to those who have allowed me to use photographs taken by them, Steve Slater, Dougie Peacock, Dave Waterman, Bill Wenger, Jay Webster and Simon Ward to name a few. My son Ross afforded me the space and solitude I needed to write, allowed me the use his computer and importantly, supplied me with endless cups of Yorkshire tea and glasses of Vino Collapso when I was flagging or losing the plot.

The biggest and heartfelt thanks however goes to my Team Commander, Major Peter Schofield. In a recent conversation with him, shortly before he passed away, he reflected on my time with the Red Devils telling me I was an extremely hard-working, loyal and talented kid and that I never let him, the Red Devils, The Parachute Regiment, the Army and importantly, myself, down. Such touching words brought tears to my eyes. There are no words to thank him for the once in a lifetime opportunity he afforded me, to pursue and achieve dreams I didn't know even existed.

Blue skies and soft landings!

Jackie

Hall of Fame

British Team 1974 – Hungary

British Team 1976 – Rome

British Team Training – Bergerac, France

British Team RW Chateauroux, France

British 8-way Team France

Aldershot Army Show – Wessex Helicopter

Meeting HRH Queen Elizabeth

Line-up for 1st Red Devil 8 and 10-way (with Golden Knight Bill Wenger)